Now in Safe Hands

Now in Safe Hands

Powerful, emotional stories

of the horses rescued by

The Devon Horse and Pony Sanctuary

Ann Diggins

Now in Safe Hands

AD PUBLISHING

First published 2019

ISBN 978-1-5272-3892-3

Printed and bound by Imprint Digital.com

DEDICATION.

This book is dedicated to Sylvia Phillips, the lady who started the Devon Horse and Pony Sanctuary in 1976. She rescued hundreds of horses over the years, from owners who abandoned, neglected or abused these beautiful animals. She went to drift sales, where Moor Ponies which had been rounded up, were destined to be sold at these meat markets and shipped abroad for slaughter. Those ponies which she rescued, lived out the rest of their lives happily and peacefully at her sanctuary.

Without her hard work and dedication, there would be no sanctuary and no happy endings. *"Saving one horse will not change the World but surely it will change the World for that one horse"*. This book is also in memory of our dear horses, who we have loved and lost.

Sylvia Phillips, pictured during one of her fund raising events.

GALLOPING ORDER

Dedication	5
Foreword	8
"A Horses Prayer"	10
How it all began: Sylvia sets up the sanctuary. Lucky's Legacy.	11
Freddie, Boris and Heathcliff's lucky escape from the Drift Sales.	21
My Story: How I became a volunteer at the sanctuary.	27
Little Humphrey breaks our hearts.	40
Comic and Copperfield: Inseparable.	54
Lewis and Joy: The show jumping horses rescued from death when their owners no longer wanted them.	64
Channel 4 Arrives at the Sanctuary.	69
Rudolph, Snowflake and Cracker: Also rescued from the Drift Sales.	73
Gallipoli: Roland's 24 hour deadline to save his life.	79
Captain and Herbie: Little and Large.	83
Deirdre, Tara and Daphne.	89

Pippin: No longer wanted by his family. 93

Cider: The one who loved cheese and onion crisps and custard creams. 98

Louis: Ex-Police Horse. Our enormous, gentle giant. 110

Fie: Abandoned by gypsies after they ruined her back legs gig racing. 115

Dolly: Worked at a riding school for disabled children in London. 142

Giselle: Our Grand Old Lady. 149

Vera: (Come in my paddock if you think you are hard enough) and Holly. 158

Snoopy:- Abandoned by gypsies in Cardiff City Centre when he was only two months old. 170

Peaches and Victor: Abandoned by gypsies. 176

Bella: Rescued from the moor when she was a tiny foal. 180

Bramble, Shannon, Buster and Miranda. 187

Staff and volunteers at Southcott: The life blood of the sanctuary. 196

Acknowledgements and thanks. 213

FOREWORD

Written by Roland and Alison Phillips, owners of the Devon Horse and Pony Sanctuary.

Ann wrote this book with mine and Alison's blessing. We are delighted that all the information and knowledge that Alison, I and some of the staff and volunteers at the Devon sanctuary have about the horses who we have been able to rescue over the years, is finally in one place.

When Ann asked us to provide details of some of the horses' backgrounds and lives, we knew we had a mammoth job ahead of us. We had a lot of information on some of the horses and not much information on a lot of them. We were able to provide the majority of this information from our memories and from our computer and old diaries, which had been kept by my mother, who started the Devon Horse and Pony Sanctuary way back in 1976.

As you might imagine, from then, up to the time Ann's work on the book came to a close in March 2019, hundreds of horses have been through our stable doors. Unfortunately, due to missing diaries and brain cells, not all the stories of the horses rescued over the years between 1976 and 2018 are included in this book.

Although only thirty-four horses' stories are told in this book, they are representative of all those other animals for whom not enough information was available about their history, to be able to include them.

Ann's book tells powerful, emotional stories of those unlucky horses who have been the subject of abandonment, dreadful neglect and abuse by cruel owners; their rescue and their arrival at our sanctuary in Devon. Alison and I are pleased to say the majority of their stories have happy endings. They really are all 'Now in Safe Hands'.

Ann is keen to provide a clear message: Don't buy a horse unless you can give it a loving 'forever home'. If your circumstances change, please do your very, very best to ensure the horse, who has given you all its love and loyalty, goes to a good, loving home.

We want to thank our present volunteers, Ann and Angie and our current full time member of staff and Manager, Micala. Our thanks also go to our previous full time members of staff and volunteers at the sanctuary. You will read later on in this book, how they have all worked together over the years and how without their support and dedication, we would not have the sanctuary we have today.

Finally, we are delighted that Ann is going to donate the proceeds of this book to the Devon Sanctuary (Charity number 280784.) If you want to know more about our work, check out our website or Facebook page. If you want to help us, please email us at:

contact@dhaps.org.uk.

Roland and Alison, with St Michael and their dog at their Sanctuary in France for retired British Police Horses.

A HORSE'S PRAYER

"Give me food and drink and care for me
when the day's work is done.
Shelter me, give me a clean bed
and leave me not too small a place in the stable.
Talk to me, for your voice often takes the place of reins,
be good to me and I will serve you yet more gladly and love you.

Don't tear at the reins, don't reach for your whip
when we come to a hill.
Don't hit me if I misunderstand you,
but give me time to understand.
Don't think me disobedient if I fail to do your will,
perhaps there is something amiss with my harness or my hooves.

Check my teeth when I don't eat,
perhaps I have a bad tooth and you know that hurts.
Don't tether me too tight and don't crop my tail,
my only weapon against mosquitoes and flies.

When the day comes, dear master,
when I am no longer any use to you,
don't let me starve or freeze, nor sell me.
Don't give me to a stranger,
who might not care for me as you have,
but be kind hearted as I would be to you."

Anon.

HOW IT ALL BEGAN:
SYLVIA SETS UP THE SANCTUARY: LUCKY'S LEGACY.

In 1976, a lady called Sylvia Phillips started a small sanctuary for unwanted horses and ponies, at her stables at Hillside, just outside the tiny village of Manaton, in Devon.

Her first rescue case was a very well-bred racehorse, originally owned by the Aga Khan. His fate was similar to that of many racehorses, once his career was over, his owners were not interested in him. He ended up in riding stables, being regularly beaten and ridden hard across Dartmoor by anybody, whether they could ride or not. If this was not bad enough, he was starved into the bargain. This eventually broke his spirit, so he was thrown out onto the moor and left to survive on his own, until Sylvia found him and took him in.

Sylvia became known as the 'mad woman from Manaton' who would take on the most distressing of horse cruelty cases. She then gave them the dignified and safe life they deserved, with no demands on them to be ridden. By 1981 she had fifty horses in her care and with the help of friends and neighbours, she formed a charity which she named: 'The Devon Horse and Pony Sanctuary'. Although small in comparison to the larger horse charities, she had the same responsibilities to ensure her horses were well fed and cared for, so she had to work very hard to raise money to keep the sanctuary afloat.

One of the ways she did this, was to have a small stall at all the local shows and events, often putting in whole days to sell her merchandise. As her reputation grew, she became very well thought of in the Equine world and was asked to be on the board for the NERC (National Equine Rescue Council).

One cold and rainy day in October 1982, Sylvia was attending the local drift sale. The Dartmoor Drift Pony Sales are a result of a centuries old practice, called 'Dartmoor Drifts.'[1] The first records of this practice date back to 1012, when cattle and ponies were rounded up three times during the summer and once during the winter months, with the purpose of ascertaining

[1] Taken from Tim Sandles' article "Dartmoor Drifts."

whether these animals were being grazed illegally on Dartmoor.

The date of the 'drift' was apparently kept a secret, so anyone who was illegally grazing their cattle or horses would be caught before they had a chance to move them on. Cattle and wild horses were rounded up separately by the tenants, who would either be on foot or horse back. The tenants were duty bound to do this, as it was written into their tenancy agreements. The rounded up animals would be taken to an agreed collection point, where the owners of the animals could collect them. Those belonging to the tenants were allowed back on the moor without any fees being charged. The owners or tenants of animals found to be grazing illegally were fined, which in those days was a 'Dunnabridge Pound' (Dunnabridge is an area near Princetown) this was the fee for grazing each animal.

Any animals which were not claimed by the owners, were taken to a local pound. This pound was owned by the Duchy and the animals were kept for twenty-one days, or until they were collected by their owners – who had to pay for the animals food and water whilst they were in the pound. For the animals which were not claimed, their fate was uncertain, as they became the property of the Duchy who sold them on at Princetown Fair and kept the money.

The old style, official Drifts, were stopped after 1940, but the sales still continue to this day, but only once a year. Unfortunately, these days, the purpose of these sales is to round up all the Dartmoor ponies and sell them to the meat traders. Ponies who are not bought for pets or by horse and pony sanctuaries are taken by lorry, to be slaughtered abroad for horse meat. At one of these drift sales, Sylvia met Nigel Nelson, a young reporter, who at that time worked for a national newspaper, the Sunday Mail.

Nigel had been asked by the paper to write a story about the drift sales in Devon and he came down to buy a pony, so he could write an accurate feature. He didn't know where to start, so he dressed in the clothes he thought were appropriate for this part of the world and tried to keep his composure as he found himself slipping and sliding around in six inches of mud. Sylvia took pity on him and offered to help him. She advised him which pony she felt needed the most help, but as he was inexperienced, he ignored her advice and spent the rest of the morning looking into each pen with her, until eventually he told her he had chosen "The One".

Sylvia looked into the pen and laughed as she told him he had chosen the one she had shown him hours before. Once Nigel had paid for the pony, she asked Nigel what he was going to do with it and by the look of shock on his face, it was obvious he hadn't thought that far ahead. Now he had to think about finding it a home and how he would get it there. Sylvia, of course, told him she would take the little pony to live at her sanctuary. He was just four months old, light brown in colour, with a lighter mane and a white blaze down his face. As he was a Dartmoor pony, he was quite small.

That weekend, the Sunday Mail ran a double page spread of Nigel's story and pictures. Readers were asked to name the pony and an appeal for money to support the sanctuary was made. The readers chose the name 'LUCKY' and the money from the appeal helped to save more Dartmoor ponies from the peril of the sales that year.

The following year, as more money was received from the Mail readers, Sylvia was able to return to the drift sales and saved six more ponies from an inevitable horrible end. As a result of the paper's continued interest over the years, money continued to flow into the Sanctuary from the general public. In addition to the money being used to care for her existing horses, this also enabled Sylvia to buy more land, to house her growing collection of rescued horses.

Some of the paddocks at the existing sanctuary at Hillside, were small and on a steep gradient, so Sylvia decided that rather than trying to expand there, she would instead buy more land at a place called Southcott, which was only a mile or two away from Hillside. This enabled her to give all the horses and ponies residing at Hillside a summer holiday, in larger, level paddocks and Sylvia was also now able to accommodate her many more new arrivals.

The horses from Hillside were taken up to Southcott each May and returned in October. Roland (Sylvia's son) and his wife Alison, remember that it was always a very exciting day when all the big horses were walked up to Southcott. They always seemed to know where they were going and couldn't wait to get there.

In 2005 when Sylvia's son Roland retired from the Metropolitan Police, he decided to help his mother out. He was worried that as the sanctuary had expanded at such a rate, it was an enormous amount of work and responsibility for one old lady. Although she had staff she employed for the heavier work, such as mucking out and doing the feeds, she ran it virtually single handed.

Due to Sylvia's failing health in 2007, the family felt she would benefit from a warmer and sunnier climate. The family decided that if they bought a small farm in the Dordogne, in the South of France, not only would Sylvia's health improve, they could also solve their problem of where to house the growing number of ex-Police horses which were now coming into their care.

Once they found a suitable property, Roland and Alison began the planning and building of purpose built stables and began to fence off paddocks which would be large enough to cater for the exercise and feeding needs of these huge ex-Police horses.

Sylvia was delighted at the prospect of being with all her beloved Police horses, which would be transported from her sanctuary in Devon, to the new Sanctuary in France. In addition to the ex-Police horses, Roland and Alison decided they would also move some of the older Devon horses over to France, if their health was failing, or if they felt the horses were too old to withstand the cold winters and changeable climate on Dartmoor. It was agreed their daughter Debbie would stay in England with her husband Chris and she would run the Devon sanctuary, with the help of the three paid members of staff, Sian, Leanne and Micala.

It is worth mentioning here how Roland came to be taking in ex-Police horses. The connection between Roland and Police horses, started when Roland joined the Metropolitan Police in 1976. He made some friends who worked in the Mounted Branch – little knowing the impact this would have on his future.

In 1993, one of the Mounted Police officers asked Roland if his mother Sylvia would take his Police horse Kendrick, as the horse couldn't be re-homed when he was retired. Roland duly visited the Mounted Branch and inspected Kendrick and agreed to take him. However, in the end two horses turned up at the Devon sanctuary, Karen and Kendrick. (These two have now both passed away.)

Word quickly spread amongst the mounted sections that

Roland's mum would take in ex-Police horses who, when due for retirement, could not be re-homed. This resulted in other branches of the Mounted Police asking if he could take their horses which they were unable to re-home.

When British Police horses have to be retired, due to age or physical or mental health reasons, the Police make strenuous efforts to find good homes for them. Their riders have built up strong, loving relationships with their horses and if they cannot offer them a home, these officers want to see their horses going to good homes, rather than be put to sleep. However, some of these horses are suffering from mental health problems, having been exposed to violent crowds, fire and rocks being thrown at them and others have physical health problems. Sometimes, this prevents them from being ridden and this makes it very difficult to find homes for them, as people prefer having a horse they can ride.

People are reticent to take on the costs of owning a very large ex-Police horse, unless there are some benefits, such as being able to ride them. Another factor which makes re-homing difficult, is that these horses don't come with a pension, in as much as none of the forces support their ex horses with financial contributions for the initial transportation costs and the other costs associated with keeping a horse.

It is a very sad fact that, having given the best part of their lives to the Force, these horses have to be destroyed if no homes can be found. However, Roland has and always will, do his very best to find room for them at his sanctuary in France.

On one occasion, Roland was contacted by the Head of one Mounted Police division on a Monday and was told a horse called Kingston was scheduled to be put down on the Thursday unless Roland could have him. Unfortunately, this was to become a familiar pattern, as Johnston and Gallipoli followed from the Metropolitan Police and then Northavon, from the Avon and Somerset mounted branch. All Police Horses face uncertain futures when they are retired, but most forces won't have the animals destroyed unless it is absolutely necessary.

Fortunately, Roland made room for all four of them, bearing the transportation and all the feeding and veterinary costs for the duration of all the ex-Police horses' lives. Northavon lived at the Brantome Sanctuary for over eighteen years, until he died recently of old age. Roland was absolutely gutted, he loves all his horses with a passion.

Sadly, Sylvia died in 2009, after devoting thirty three years of her life to the rescue and rehabilitation of hundreds of horses, ponies and donkeys. Her favourites by far were the Police horses, who she used to call her 'Gentlemen'.

Roland tells me their fundraising in France totalled £24,000 in 2014 and £30,000 in 2015. These vital funds pay for feeds, farrier, hay, vet and dental treatment for the sanctuaries in Devon and France. Bills for our Devon sanctuary alone in 2014, were over three thousand pounds. Roland and Alison hold open days at their Brantome sanctuary and money is also raised by putting on cream teas, summer balls and they organise a massive Christmas Fair each year with over five hundred people attending the last one.

They also have a purpose built room next to the stables, where their visitors are shown a short film of some of their ex-Police horses, during their time on active duty. A small gift shop is now open, where visitors can purchase small gifts which tops up the well needed funds.

If I am ever unable to get hold of either Alison or Roland, I know it is because Alison is up to her eyes either baking cakes for the cream teas, cooking meals for their evening fund raising events or organising future events. I reckon Alison could give Mary Berry a run for her money on who bakes the best cakes. Roland is, as always, hands-on looking after the horses.

The French Sanctuary has now become known as 'Brantome Police Horses & Friends'. There are, at the time of writing, twenty two equines residing there and you can read more about the horses there and the work Roland and Alison do, by visiting either their Facebook page, or their Web site. Their sanctuary is well worth a visit if you are ever on holiday in France and near the area. I believe they are still the number one visitor attraction in the Brantome area on TripAdvisor.

The Devon Horse and Pony Sanctuary is also a registered charity and we rely on four sources of income: The money raised over in France, the public's generosity here in England (who give us donations), the money still being generated by the newspaper article about Lucky all those years ago and legacies.

So, returning to Lucky. He settled in very well on his arrival at the sanctuary in October 1982. In 1990, a little Exmoor/Shetland pony, called Robin arrived, with another Shetland called Rosie. When Sylvia examined Robin, apart from his hooves which had overgrown, she found poor Robin had cataracts in both eyes and was virtually blind. His companion Rosie was his eyes and he would follow her everywhere. When Rosie died, Robin was not left to cope on his own very long, as Lucky immediately took over and they became constant companions.

Lucky became Robin's eyes and they were never far from each other. If ever Robin wandered off and became disorientated, he would call out to Lucky and Lucky would call back and go straight over to his friend and guide him back. During my time at the sanctuary, I once witnessed a very touching episode with Robin and Lucky. It was the day a horse called Pippin arrived at Southcott, having just been returned from Roland and Alison's sanctuary in France. Sian decided to put him in a paddock with, amongst others, Robin and Lucky. Understandably, Pippin was nervous, unsettled and frightened after his long journey. When the other horses came over to say "hi", he turned his back on them and lashed out with his back legs.

Poor Robin, oblivious to the danger of Pippin's close proximity, received a hefty kick to his side. He panicked and called out for Lucky. Lucky immediately ran over and put himself between Pippin and Robin, despite the fact he was much smaller than Pippin. I could hardly believe what I had just seen, but there was no doubt that Lucky was protecting Robin. Sian and I agreed we could not risk any of the sanctuary horses being injured, especially our 'oldies', so we moved Pippin out of that paddock.

When I first clapped eyes on Lucky, in 2011, I made the assumption that as he was very old, he would be quite placid, easy to lead and easy to handle. Not so! He was a real character and very wilful - if he didn't want to be led somewhere, he would stand fast and nothing would shift him. When he trod on my foot one day, I was in agony for hours – how could such a small horse be so heavy? It was a lesson to be learned for me and after that, I watched my feet all the time, especially around the bigger horses.

Poor old Lucky was starting to wear out early in 2014. At his ripe old age, that was only to be expected, but we all hoped he would soldier on. He suffered from weepy eyes and at one stage the vet was called out to treat an ulcer in his eye. He became very thin, but was well looked after by all of us at the sanctuary, receiving regular grooms and sometimes Sian walked him and Robin to Manaton and back.

During cold, wet winters, he was rugged up and stabled at night during the worst of the weather, with his best friend Robin. This was mainly to ensure they didn't fall over in the mud at night and either die from their exertions of trying to get up or hyperthermia. I always worry about all the horses at the sanctuary in the winter months, especially the old ones. My partner reminded me once that I was working at the horse version of an old peoples' home. She is right of course and yes, we expect losses, but they are still so very hard to bear.

Lucky soldiered on until the morning of 15th March, 2015 when Sian found him laying down in his stable and was unable to get him up. She called Kevin, our vet out, who said he felt Lucky was tired and had had enough of life and it would be kinder to put him to sleep. Lucky passed away quietly, his head cradled in Sian's arms. He was 32 and a very special little pony who would be so sadly missed, not only by his friend Robin, but all of us as well. He is a legend as far as all of us at the Sanctuary are concerned and has created a legacy that the charity will always be grateful for.

It made our hearts ache further when Robin was still calling for Lucky weeks after his death. Sadly, no other horse took him under their wing, so he got special treatment from all of us. I found it so sad to see him standing on his own, because although he had the company of two other 'oldies', Jess and Bonnie Bella (you will read about them in later chapters) they did not care for him like Lucky did. We don't know how old Robin was, but he was probably well on the way to being 40 years old. Despite being blind, he found his way around and astounded us all with his courage and tenacity.

Robin surprised us all by living another couple of years. Sadly, he collapsed on 2nd February, 2017 and Sian called the vet out. He diagnosed heart problems and advised Sian that due to his age and the condition of his heart, it would be kinder to put him to sleep. It was a very sad day, saying goodbye to our longest resident and he is still missed.

We continue to work hard at our Devon Sanctuary to give all our residents and new arrivals the safe, secure and loving environment they deserve. The following chapters in this book tell these horses' stories.

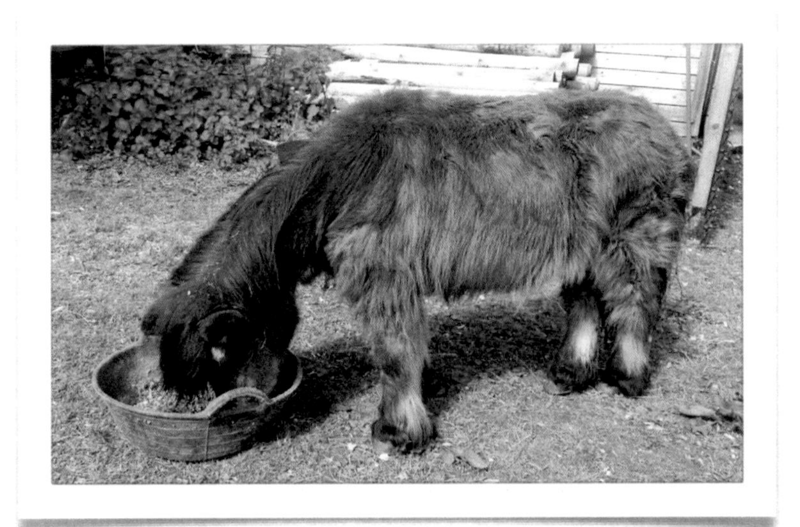

Robin enjoying his first feed of the day.

Sian, kneeling down with Lucky (his mate Robin in background). Stabled in bad weather.

Freddie

FREDDIE'S, BORIS'S AND HEATHCLIFF'S LUCKY ESCAPE FROM THE DRIFT SALES.

Freddie was born in 1992 and lived as a wild pony on Dartmoor, Devon. He was first seen by Roland's mother Sylvia, hanging around the car park of a popular tourist spot called Widecombe-in-the-Moor, with his mother.

At that time, Freddie was a four month old adorable foal and he and the other ponies there made a good living cadging treats and ice-creams from holiday makers. Sylvia fell in love with Freddie and vowed that if she ever saw him at the Drift Pony Sales, she would give him a good home at the Sanctuary for life.

That autumn, Freddie (along with Heathcliff and Boris, who were also around four months old) was rounded up for the Dartmoor Drift sales at Ashburton, which are held every year in October. They found themselves amongst the many horses and ponies which would be bought for meat - for just a few guineas each. They would then begin a torturous journey when they were shipped off for slaughter on the Continent.

The guinea[2] was minted in Great Britain between 1663 and 1814 and was made out of a quarter of an ounce of gold. During that period, it was worth one pound; which was around twenty shillings in old money. Even when our currency changed to decimalisation, the guinea continued to be used well into the 20th century, being worth £1.05. It was mainly used by the horse community, either during horse racing or at the drift sales.

Sylvia was at this particular drift sale early, as she was very anxious in case she missed Freddie going through the sale ring. Her plan was to stand where she was in full sight of the ring, but where she could also see the transporters outside. Unfortunately, because the ring was so packed with these terrified ponies, she missed him. However, relief flooded through her when she suddenly picked him out amongst many other ponies being led up the ramp to one of the lorries. If it were not for his striking bright chestnut colour, she could have easily have missed him

---

2 Wikipedia

and the thought of that made her feel sick. Her heart in her mouth, she ran as quickly as she could to the transporter and once she caught her breath, she offered the trader money for him. He sold Freddie to her on the spot, for five pounds so she dashed up the ramp and brought him back out.

Whilst negotiating with the trader, Sylvia also spotted Heathcliff and Boris. She couldn't resist those two either, so she bought them as well and set about arranging transport to take all three of them back to her Sanctuary. The three lucky new ones joined the herd of existing ponies that Sylvia had saved from slaughter over the years. They went on to enjoy many happy years together in the company of their new friends. Freddie was a great hit with visiting children, because of his sweet and friendly nature and was always very popular with adults too. Heathcliff went out on loan to a family, but was returned later in his life and spent the rest of his days with Boris and the others at the Southcott sanctuary.

Sadly, Freddie became prone to a dreadful disease called Laminitis. This disease cannot be cured but can be managed with care and careful husbandry. Laminitis[3] is one of the most serious, crippling and agonizing diseases horses, ponies and donkeys can experience.

It is a painful inflammatory condition of the laminae tissues which are found in the horses hoof. It can affect any horse, of any age or sex, at any time of the year. However, horses are more prone to this in the spring, when they eat too much new, fresh grass which contains more sugar. Severe and recurring cases of laminitis can result in the horse being destroyed to prevent further suffering.

When one of our horses is diagnosed with Laminitis, we class this as an emergency and our vet is called out immediately. Immediate treatment is critical and can reduce the effects of laminitis. The horse needs to be stabled with a deep bed of shavings immediately. Painkillers are usually given and in some cases 'frog supports' (to support the foot). The horse will then be put on a 'forage based' diet which is limited to a mixture of mature grass, and water soaked hay with Alfalfa. Alfalfa

---

[3] Source – 'Animed Veterinary Hospital and Equine Unit' Web page.

contains essential minerals and proteins that the horse can utilize to improve hoof quality. Plenty of water should be available to assist digestion and to avoid colic.

During Freddie's stay at our Devon sanctuary, there are various diary entries about him being a "bit light, so give more hay", to him not being very well in 2011 and having to go into the 'starvation paddock' as he was getting 'lumpy and lazy'. This may have been a reference to his Laminitis. At one stage, he was wearing Frog supports as he was lame.

During Christmas 2008, a new foal, Cracker had arrived at the Devon Sanctuary, having been rescued from the drift sales with two Dartmoor ponies', Rudolph and Snowflake. Freddie immediately took Cracker under his wing, acting like a surrogate father. They became the best of friends and as the days and weeks progressed, they became inseparable. (See the chapter on Rudolph, Snowflake and Cracker for more details on Cracker.)

When Cracker was put in with him, Freddie was soon cantering around and we think that as he was using more energy doing this, he lost a bit of weight and was soon on the mend. When Freddie's laminitis became more frequent, it was a major cause for concern. Roland and Alison decided to have him transported to their Police Horse Sanctuary in the Dordogne, France, where he could be carefully monitored. Of course his best friend Cracker had to go with him.

So, on the fourteenth of April, 2012, our vet Kevin came up to Southcott, to carry out the usual checks horses must go through, prior to transportation to France (these are discussed in the Chapter 'Channel Four Arrives'). Freddie and Cracker left on the transporter for France the next day, with instructions that as Freddie was asthmatic, he must have haylage, not hay in the transport lorry, as hay was too dusty. As they disappeared up the ramp of the transporter, heading for their new life in France, they looked splendid wearing their new head collars. Freddie and Cracker would be a good attraction for the younger visitors to the French sanctuary, Freddie in particular has a gentle and friendly personality and is always kind to people. He loves children and attention.

Roland is sure that his mother Sylvia, had she been alive to see it, would have been really pleased that Freddie had made it to France to live out his days in their sanctuary. She would have been delighted to know that he is now enjoying a happy life surrounded by all his old ex-Police horse friends and of course, his beloved Cracker.

The girls at the Sanctuary always said it was sometimes a struggle to tell the difference between Boris and Cracker. However, as Boris had white 'eye brow' shape markings above his eyes, it was reasonably easy to spot the difference providing you could see these.

By the time I had begun to work at the sanctuary in 2011, Heathcliff was in his advancing years, but he was almost impossible to catch when it was time to move him and his mates to another paddock. In addition, Heathcliff seemed to have a sixth sense and knew when it was farrier day, so no one could catch him not even with his favourite mints. On the majority of occasions, the farrier would have to chase him around and rugby tackle him to the ground, which was very entertaining, unless you were the farrier.

What was not funny for me to watch, was the day he and his other pint sized mates decided it would be fun to chase my dog Milo around their paddock. They might have been little, but what they lacked in size, they made up for in speed and aggression. They had poor Milo cornered in no time and I had to run over waving a poo picker at them to get them to back off.

Heathcliff also suffered from laminitis, but not on the same scale as Freddie. When this occurred, Heathcliff was stabled and put on a restricted diet for a few weeks and was given pain killers in the form of sachets of Bute. One time, our donkey Miranda had to be stabled with him, as he reacted badly to being on his own.

Off and on during 2011, Heathcliff continued to suffer with Laminitis. His legs appeared sore and he was sometimes found lying down when the girls arrived. During that period, our vet Kevin was called out to him, but the result was always the same – stabled, restricted diet and pain killers. Laminitis is a killer, so we had to be very careful with him. In the end, it was not laminitis that finished off our beloved Heathcliff. He passed away on New Year's Day, 2014. He had a heart murmur and subsequently died of a heart attack.

Boris, Freddie and Cracker at Southcott, with Dolly behind

Following Heathcliff's death, Boris, his faithful companion was then teamed up with Pippin, but not for long. I was to experience my first dying horse on 18th March, 2014. As Karen and I pulled up at the entrance gate to the sanctuary, I looked down into the small paddock and was horrified to see Boris flat out looking lifeless.

As we had lost quite a few horses in the beginning of 2014, I think I instinctively knew as I raced towards him, that he was not long for this world. I could see by the flatness of the ground around him that he had been down all night and he was exhausted. Even as I knelt down beside him, I could tell by his eyes he was in big trouble and he was too weak to get up.

I rang the vet immediately and then dashed up to the barn to get some spare rugs to put under his head and on top of him to keep him warm. I spent the rest of the time between then and when Kevin arrived, sitting down cradling Boris's head on my lap, stroking and talking to him.

I could see by Kevin's face when he had examined Boris that he was going to put him to sleep. Due to all that trauma, I can't remember what Kevin diagnosed Boris with, but I think it was a twisted gut. As the lethal blue liquid flowed into Boris' veins, he slipped away quietly with me stroking his head, which had remained on my lap.

I was very traumatised by all this. It was the first time I had seen one of our horses put to sleep. I was therefore in floods of tears when I rang Roland to let him know what had happened. Another one gone, the only consolation was he had a lovely life. I was also relieved Sian did not have to find Boris, as she had already gone through the trauma of finding so many of our horses in trouble on her arrival that year.

MY STORY: HOW I BECAME A VOLUNTEER AT THE SANACTUARY.

My cousin Susan had taught me to look after and ride horses when I was very young in the early sixties and growing up in Essex. Susan was horse mad and since we got on really well, I decided I wanted to spend as much time as I could with her and her horses during school holidays. She was at the stables from early in the morning until late afternoon, so I nagged her until I got myself invited. This was to awaken a deep and lasting love of horses in me.

I was only about eleven, still in pig tails. I remember being quite daunted by the size of some of the horses up there, especially Susan's. Tina was a highly strung dark chestnut horse, whom Susan adored. I was taught how to muck out the stables, groom and feed her horses. I gradually began to feel comfortable around them and my days up there were precious and happy. Packing up our lunch for the day was exciting, my anticipation heightened by the prospect of my being with the horses I was becoming very attached to.

My comfort was short lived when Susan decided it was time for me to learn to ride. She picked, what was to me, a massive horse called Tony. He was a white Welsh cob and I could barely get my legs round him. He was what you might call a 'steady horse' although one incident still stays in my mind. We were in a small paddock behind the barn and I was learning to trot round the paddock. One minute things were going well, the next, he was bolting for the massive double doors, which lead into the huge barn.

Unfortunately, these double doors opened outwards and were barely open now. As we shot over to these doors, I shut my eyes and braced myself. He got through, but the doors hit me, so I was knocked off in the process. Sue made me get back on immediately, although I was shaken and upset.

As time went by, I was allowed to ride Susan's horse, Tina. She was leaner than Tony, so more comfortable to ride, although I had to be constantly on my guard for things which might make her spook and throw me off. I never did fall off again, so I suppose this is testament to how well Susan taught me to ride. I don't remember riding outside the stables, but it was a massive place, so I think there was plenty of room for a learner to increase their skills in trotting, cantering and galloping round the paddocks.

When I think back to my childhood, the time with the horses is one of my favourite memories and I have Susan to thank for instigating my love of horses and wanting to be near them, which continues to this day. Sadly, all too soon, these idyllic times came to an end when Susan started dating and suddenly had priorities other than her horses.

During the years that followed, I was to experience a quite a bit of moving around within Essex, then to Hertfordshire. However, the biggest and for me, most unwelcome change came in 1970, when I was eighteen. Always in pursuit of promotion, my father came home one evening and announced he had put in for a job in Cornwall. We had holidayed there a lot over the years and my dad was keen to move us out of London, into a better environment. My mum was delighted but I was horrified. Cornwall was lovely for holidays, but live there? At first, I refused to accept the idea, until my dad, very cleverly told me if I moved down to Cornwall with no further fuss, he would buy me a car. We moved down in September of that year and it was through my first job that I came into contact with someone who would introduce me back into riding within a few months.

My first job was with a company called SWEB (South Western Electricity Board) in a small office in Liskeard, a few miles from where we lived in Dobwalls. I began what was to become a long and successful career, as an Office Staff Trainee and as such had to spend a few weeks in different departments to learn the business. During this time, I became friendly with a lady called Francis. Her husband John was a Lieutenant in the Royal Navy, serving on the Ark Royal. They lived in a very small village called Crow's Nest, a few miles outside of Liskeard.

During one of our many conversations, Francis mentioned her husband was looking for someone to exercise his two horses, whilst he was away at sea. I explained to her that I was taught to ride at a young age, but I was very rusty as I hadn't had any contact with horses since then.

Francis invited me over to their bungalow at Crow's Nest

when John was home on leave. I was to meet him and go out for a 'test' ride, so he could see whether I was too rusty to be able to handle his two horses. Being a Lieutenant in the Royal Navy he cut a dashing figure and he also had very high standards when it came to riding. I must admit, at the tender age of eighteen, I was a little over awed by him. We rode out the same week and I quickly learnt that it was not acceptable for me to turn up in jeans, wellies and an old anorak.

I was dispatched to the local shops to buy jodhpurs, riding hat, boots and jacket. I pretended to be put out by this, but was secretly very happy showing off my new gear. John homed my riding skills on Trooper, a massive black Welsh Cobb, who was very steady, sure footed and had a very gentle temperament. John rode Lady Francis, another huge, but nervy thoroughbred horse, who was frightened of her own shadow. She used to refuse to walk through puddles or past corrugated iron. Old plastic carrier bags flapping about in hedges were also life threatening. John taught me not to give in to this behaviour, so our rides were often delayed while one of us battled to get her past these obstacles. He also taught me that in these circumstances, you had more control of the horse if you were on it, as opposed to leading it. As a result, when I graduated to riding Lady Francis, I spent a lot of time learning how to stay on this skittish horse, who danced and bucked around inanimate objects and puddles she feared were dangerous.

As the weeks and months of my tuition went on, I was able to progress comfortably on Trooper from slow walks and trots across the moors and round country lanes, to full throttle gallops on the moor. John never seemed content unless we rode like our back-sides were on fire, over all sorts of terrain, dodging boulders, plunging down small ravines and over gorse bushes. Many times I fell off and many times, like my cousin in my younger days, he made me get back on, crying or not. At no time during all this, do I remember being worried before a ride, or afraid during one. I used to look forward to each ride out. Amazingly, I never injured myself either.

Once, on the way back from a long ride, we were returning through the very narrow lanes which led to Crow's Nest, when a car hammered past. I was riding Lady Francis (by then I had been deemed to be competent enough to ride her for the duration of the whole ride) and in her fear, she tried to jump up on top of a high hedge. I am still not sure to this day how I didn't fall off (probably a testament to John's good tuition) but I remember John throwing his crop at the car's back window, such was his fury.

John wanted me to go hunting with him, as he said I was now a very competent rider and would enjoy the challenges of the ride. Hunting was the only thing we ever argued over – I was (and still am) very anti-hunt and nothing he said, could convince me to change my mind. My mum always said it was the "unspeakable going after the uneatable." I agree with her sentiment that if there was no showing off involved in the form of dressing up and meeting up outside pubs, this barbaric practice would die out.

One fox against many hounds, which I have been told are starved days prior to the hunt does not seem fair to me. Particularly, as prior to a hunt, all badger and fox holes in the area will be blocked up by the terrier men and I have been told some hunts catch foxes from out of the area and release them just as the hunt rides out. These poor creatures have no idea where they are and have no chance of escaping down a hole. They end up being ripped apart by starving hounds. I cannot understand the mentality of people who think this is good fun and a great sport. Even though hunting is illegal, it continues to this day with little Police intervention.

When John went to sea, I enlisted my best mate Cynthia to come out riding with me. As long as we cleaned tack and mucked out the stables, John was happy for us to ride as often as we liked, so we rode every day. We had races up 'Fore Down' an area of the moor just outside Crow's Nest. We rode for hours on the moor, around the village of Minions, where we would tie our horses up outside the Cheese Wring pub and enjoy a ploughman's lunch with a small beer, before setting off again.

Once, when we were racing across the moors, the girth on my saddle broke. Somehow, I got the saddle out from beneath me and discarded it, not wanting to stop as I was winning our race. It meant I had to go back for it, but that was worth the jubilation

Cynthia with Trooper before one of our rides. Note the attire.

of winning our race and I felt proud I had ridden the last few hundred yards bare back at break neck speed.

Once we had returned the horses to their stables in Crow's Nest, de-tacked and rubbed them down, we would ride them bare back through the village to their paddock, steering with just a lead reign attached to their head collars.

Somewhere in the middle of all this amazing fun, Francis was killed in a car accident. She had left our office to go home for lunch and never came back. This really upset me, as I had become very fond of her and poor John was devastated. He left the navy shortly afterwards, so we went riding more regularly. As well as riding with him, I became part of his social clique, dinner parties and pub crawls round Liskeard, Looe and other neighbouring villages. I ended up falling in love with him and I was absolutely devastated when he acquired a new lady friend called Pat. I was determined not to like her, but she was a lovely, caring, warm person and clearly madly in love with John. She quickly won me over and we became firm friends, regularly riding out together. They were married within the year.

I lost touch with them when, in 1978, I left home to move up to Plymouth, as a result of promotion within SWEB. My life changed quite radically – with the new job, came new friends and new interests.

Many years later, in 2009, I was sitting at my desk in my office, when Jeff, one of my three managers who worked for me in my team, came in waving a newspaper clipping at me. "Ann, here is something you can do when you retire. This is an article in the Daily Mail, about a horse sanctuary on Dartmoor." Jeff knew I loved horses so had kindly saved it for me. I kept that article for many years and am so thankful to him for bringing that in, as it was to open up a whole new life for me.

It was in the summer of 2011, just over a year after I retired at fifty seven, when I looked for the article Jeff had brought in for me. I went on the Devon Horse and Pony Sanctuary web site and read about the horses and the work the staff did. They seemed to have a mixture of breeds of horses from different backgrounds, which had suffered varying levels of mistreatment - abandonment, cruelty or both.

I was a little concerned about contacting the charity, because although I had been taught to ride and look after horses at a young age in the early sixties, I had had no further contact with horses until the early seventies. Compared to the other girls working at the sanctuary, I knew I had little experience. Joining the sanctuary would be my first contact with horses for over forty years.

Pushing my concerns aside, I eventually summoned up the courage to email the Sanctuary. I was honest and said although I loved horses, I hadn't been around them for many years, but did know how to look after them. Debbie, the owners' daughter, emailed me back and asked if I could meet her, so she could show me around the sanctuary. She arranged to meet me at the village green, in the tiny village of Manaton. She explained the Sanctuary was a few miles away from the village, reached by driving up some very narrow lanes. It would be easier if I followed her there.

On 16th July, 2011, I navigated my way up to Bovey Tracey from Plymouth and turned off just outside the small town, to begin the steady five mile climb up to the top of the moors. The scenery was stunning, panoramic views for miles. To this day, some eight years later, I still appreciate what a beautiful part of the world I live in.

I was, of course, early. I amuse all my friends by being early for important events. When we go on holiday, I always stay overnight the day before our flight, near the airport. I know of too many people who have driven up to Gatwick or Heathrow on the same day they are due to fly and missed their flights, due to accidents on the motorway resulting in huge tail backs.

As I sat in the car by Manaton Green, waiting for Debbie, I was very nervous. I had plenty of time to worry about what it would be like, being around horses again. Would I have forgotten things? Would I be nervous of them? What would the staff think of me? My main concern was around whether they would think I was good enough to look after their horses. My stomach was churning as I waited and I cursed my desire to be early for everything.

Debbie was not joking when she said the sanctuary was reached by narrow lanes. I was driving my new pride and joy, a retirement present to myself, my Audi S3. I think I actually drove those last few miles behind Debbie holding my breath. The lanes were narrower than anything I had ever driven down, with stones jutting out of the walls and brambles growing out of them. To make matters worse, because Debbie knew those lanes like the back of her hand, she hurtled up them at an alarming speed and had to wait for me to catch up more than once.

When I arrived at the sanctuary, the stunning views took my breath away. It was beautiful, surrounded by farmers' fields, with views of the moors and forests in the distance. The sanctuary was literally in the middle of nowhere. It had four stables and an old stone barn, which was used to store the horse feed and associated equipment, including feeding bowls, feed bins, head collars and much more. The yard was just a small area of grass in front of the stables, but it was love at first sight for me.

Debbie showed me round all the paddocks and I met all the horses. She told me their histories, their names and how they had come to be up here. Blimey, how on earth would I remember all that? We spent a few hours talking, during which time I suppose she was assessing whether or not I would make volunteer material. There were three full time employees there – Sian, Micala and Lianne. I asked about other volunteers, but was told: "They never last." At the time, I was not sure whether that was a challenge, or a sad fact, but I was determined to be the one who stayed. What's not to like? Horses, fresh air, stunning countryside.

I must have given them a good impression, because I was asked to come up one day a week and 'be trained' by one of the other girls. When and if they decided I was good enough to go up on my own, I would be trusted to do so. So that is how it all started. Wednesdays were allocated as my days. Of course, I decided I had to have the right 'gear' (probably the influence of Johns' rules all those years ago.) So after my second visit, I raided Mole Valley Farmers on the way home and bought riding boots (with enforced toe area), a new horsey top, a long water proof coat and a body warmer.

My partner had been very pleased when I said I was going to contact the charity and volunteer to help. She was very relieved I was not going to help out at the local cats and dogs home in Plymouth, which, she said, would have resulted in my giving in to temptation and coming home with more animals. "You can't bring a horse home" she said with confidence. Not quite, but later, I ended up adopting a horse called Fie, who had arrived just weeks before me. You will read about her later in this book.

I bought a small red note book to take up with me on my next visit, so I could write down the names of all the horses and what chores needed doing each day. I also recorded that Micala had two, two year old girls and Sian was very young herself with a new baby, called Lola. Leanne had a Range Rover and a hunting horn as ring tone on her mobile. That used to make my blood run cold.

The horses there at that time which went in my little red note book were: Lewis (ex-international show jumper); Gallipoli (ex-Police horse); Miranda the donkey; Deirdre (small grey mare); Vera (girls called her "vicious Vera"); Freddie (the one with Laminitis) Robin (the little blind Shetland); Lucky (the very old one, Robin's best mate); the new Bay Fiesta; Copperfield (large Shire Horse); Comic (Large Hunter). The small Dartmoor ponies were Holly, Cracker, Boris (so called because of big white 'eye brow shaped' markings above his eye) and Heathcliff.

The list of chores I wrote in my red note book were as follows:

- On arrival, visit all paddocks/fields and make sure all horses ok.
- Check diary in barn to see what has been written over the previous week and if there is anything specific to do.
- Feed horses as per instructions in diary.
- Fill used hay nets before leaving.
- Check water containers in paddocks.
- Clean poo out of stables, sweep back remaining bedding, adding clean if necessary.
- Check water in stables and put fresh in if necessary.
- Poo pick fields and shelters.
- Put Citronella cream on horses' faces to deter flies.
- Comic's ointment for cut.
- Apply any other vet creams as instructed in diary.
- Pick out hooves.
- Groom in summer/groom any in stables.

Other notes I made included: "When leading a horse, always stand on level with the flank, NOT IN FRONT of the horse." In later years, I was to become a little complacent doing that and as a result, ended up in casualty. You will read about that in Fie's chapter. There is also a diagram in my little red book for how I was to do a 'D' knot when tying up a hay net, notes on how to put a halter on and how to tell if a horse is cold. Some say feel the backs of their ears, others, under their stomach.

Following around eight Wednesdays worth of 'training', I was allowed to go 'solo'. On the day of my first solo shift, I was very nervous on the journey up. Not sure why, as I only had a few chores to do. Firstly, I had to feed Robin and Lucky, our very small Shetland ponies. This involved catching them and leading them into the yard. Not much to worry about there, because Robin was blind and Lucky was very old. Whilst they ate, the next job was to walk round and inspect all the other horses, doing hands on checks, to make sure they were ok and not injured in any way. I then poo picked the appropriate paddocks and shelters and ensured all the troughs and other containers had water in them. Then, I returned Robin and Lucky to their paddock. Simples!

When I had finished, I up dated our diary, which was kept in the barn. Although I had thoroughly enjoyed being up at the sanctuary, I was very relieved my first solo shift had passed without incident and that I hadn't made any mistakes. I often wonder if one of the girls went up there later to check I had done all I was supposed to and had locked the gate properly. Can't blame them if they did. Little did they know, that as I have mild OCD, leaving gates open or unlocked is not something I would ever do. Quite regularly, after my shift, I would get down to the village and a little voice in my head would ask me if I had chained up and padlocked the front gate. I knew I had, but all the same, I had to go back up. The gate was, of course, always padlocked.

I mentioned that we kept a daily diary, which was left in the barn. The girls made entries of what they did at the sanctuary each day and wrote instructions for the person on the next shift. I was to get plenty of 'tellings-off' via this diary. My first was when, after six months or so, I moved Vera out of the paddock she shared with Fie, as Vera was bullying her. Written in the next day's page in capital letters and underlined many times (in a fit of anger no doubt) was **"NEVER PUT A HORSE ON ITS OWN IN A PADDOCK. DO NOT MOVE HORSES AROUND WITHOUT ASKING FIRST."** Fair enough.

I was in trouble again about a year later, being told (in capital letters again) to **"READ UP ON LAMINITIS ANN."** I knew I had a lot to learn, but grew tired of the method of these tellings-off, so I put a polite note in the diary to the effect that if they had a problem with something I had done, I would prefer a phone call. This was too much like being in school! I appreciated I had to be pulled up when I did something wrong, but this needed to be done verbally, so at least I got an explanation of why it was wrong.

So it turned out, I was the one volunteer who stayed. I have racked up more years up there than the past and present full time staff. I am into my eighth year now and I am still spending every Wednesday up there and most weeks in the summer, I go up an additional day to see Fie. I also do other days or weekends if necessary, to cover for any of the staff who are on holiday. I estimate that over the years, I have clocked up approximately 25,500 miles, spending £6,700 on petrol and that is only on the basis of a once a week visit and does not include all the extra days of cover I have done for holidays. I have worked through the worst of the winter weather Dartmoor can throw at me, but on a summers' day I can't think of anywhere else I would rather be. Leanne and Micala left a year after I started to pursue other jobs. However, I am delighted that Micala has recently made a very welcome return to the sanctuary. Her experience with horses is invaluable and she has a great way with them.

When I am shovelling horse poo into wheel barrows and labouring up a muddy, slippery field in the pouring, driving rain, funnily enough, Jeff pops into my head – smiling and waving that newspaper clipping at me. It is also at this time, that I often think of some of my friends who's hobbies include art, keep fit and other indoor pursuits and wonder (but only briefly) why I do this back breaking, knackering work and worse still, have my heart broken when one of our horses dies. The answer is simple. I love these horses.

Whatever the weather, even if it is a dry day, the physical work is still very tiring. Wheeling a wheel barrow full of feeding bowls with full hay nets balanced on the top, across a paddock potted with dips and ruts is very challenging. Made worse when my dog frequently drops his ball in front of the wheelbarrow, causing it to tip over.

In the summer, we all spend more time at the sanctuary. When the chores are done, we catch up on other things like mending fences, hacking back hedges and creosoting. However, the absolute best thing about having warm sunny and dry weather, is the fact it allows us to groom the horses and just be with them. They love the attention. Some of my friends think I am mad, but there is nowhere else I would rather be on a nice day, or on a horrible day as well, come to that. I am the equivalent of a baby bore with my horses. When I am not up there, I am either thinking about them or talking about them. I wake up in the night worrying about them if the weather is awful. Fie is normally the first thing I think about when I wake up.

The rewards of working up at the sanctuary far outweigh the physical pain and heart break. Plus, in the winter, there is always a hot bath with a large 'brandy floater' (my own invention – a glass of brandy and Lovage, floating around in the hot water) to look forward to upon arriving home. In the summer, it's a well-deserved pint in the garden.

A few years ago, Sian asked me if I wanted to go out riding with her. She had two horses and said she would ride the smaller of the two. She asked when I had last ridden and I must admit I was a little economical with the truth and told a white lie. I said I had ridden about five or six years ago. I didn't want to spoil my chances of getting on a horse again, although I was very nervous at the mere thought of it.

I immediately arranged to go to some local stables, near Bickleigh, just outside Plymouth. I wanted to make sure I hadn't forgotten anything. During the first session they put me on a horse and asked me to perform basic movements in a small paddock, which I passed with flying colours. After all those years, I hadn't forgotten anything. The following week, I went out on a 1-2-1 basis with an instructor for an hours ride. It was wonderful to be back in the saddle again.

Following another three weeks of riding at Bickleigh, I felt confident enough to go out riding with Sian. I was quite nervous, but we only walked through country lanes, near where she has her horses, just outside Kingsteignton. She was kind enough to give me some tips as we went, but as she didn't ask me again, I suppose she thought my riding wasn't up to much.

To work around our horses at the sanctuary, you need guts, compassion, patience, lots of love and understanding, a sense of humour and sometimes lots of tissues and a cuddle with a fellow human being.

As the years have gone by, emotionally, I have found it harder to be at the sanctuary. When I first started to go up there in July 2011, the horses were just names. As the months rolled by, they became dear to me. I came to know their personalities and the more I loved them, the more difficult it became when one fell ill and it was absolutely heart breaking when one died.

The motto of the owner of the Sanctuary, Roland, is: "The only predictable thing about horses, is the fact they are unpredictable." My mottos are: Never get sandwiched between a horse and a gate or a wall. Watch their feet and yours and finally, always look at their ears – forewarned is forearmed.

If I could send out a message to the readers of this book, it would be to think very hard and carefully before buying a horse, or taking one out on loan. We see too many horses who are the product of owners who cannot or do not want to keep them anymore. This is normally due to the fact the children have out grown them, their owners move house and cannot find land to keep them on, or just cannot afford to keep them. Horses have feelings and it must be hard and hurtful for them to be discarded whatever the reason. Why not work at a horse sanctuary and get the best of both worlds?

Milo with the ball which caused so many over turned wheelbarrows

LITTLE HUMPHREY BREAKS OUR HEARTS.

As she drove past the water filled ditch at the side of a main road in Cardiff, the woman did a double take. What was that, lying flat out, nearly submerged, in the icy water? It looked like an animal and it was much larger than a dog. She had no idea what it could be and was filled with dread, as she knew she had to pull over and find out. She would not be able to live with herself if she drove past and just hoped that someone else would stop. The traffic was very heavy, yet she saw no cars slow down, let alone stop to look at the water logged animal, to see if they might help. As these thoughts raced through her head, her car was slowing and angry motorists jolted her out of her dilemma by sounding their horns. She made her decision, she had no choice but to stop and take responsibility for rescuing whatever it was.

She quickly pulled over and snatched her mobile out of her bag and ran back to the ditch. She was sure whatever it was, was dead, but what if it wasn't?

Her heart hammering, she approached the body and saw it was a very young horse. He was emaciated, his long coat matted and waterlogged. His eyes were closed and his body looked lifeless. She wondered if the little horse had escaped from his home because he had a head collar on or whether he had just been abandoned.

She was sure he was dead, but was too frightened to approach the body in case this poor creature was alive, as she knew nothing about horses and was very nervous of them. With shaking hands, she rang the Police for advice as to what she should do. The Police said they would send someone immediately and they would also contact the Horse Warden and assured her that they would be there as soon as they could.

The woman stood nervously near the body, which had not stirred and wondered if she should try and put a blanket over the poor animal to try and keep it warm, in case it was alive. A quick search of her car revealed she had nothing appropriate and she was on her way back to the horse when the Police and the Cardiff City Horse Warden arrived.

The more experienced Horse Warden was not afraid to approach the horse and following a short examination, she saw a tiny sign of life and immediately rang the local vet. She also arranged transportation for the weak horse, to warm, safe and secure premises. The Horse Warden wanted to try and get the horse out of the icy water as soon as possible, concerned that the longer he stayed in the water, the less likely he was to survive. While they waited for the vet and the horse box to arrive she asked the Police and the lady if they would be able to help get the poor horse out of the water filled ditch and back on his feet. This was going to be an almost impossible task, because the little horse was close to death with cold and starvation and he was heavy because the water had soaked into his thick coat.

Eventually, the group of rescuers managed to drag the horse out of the ditch and amazingly, coax him to his feet. The Warden immediately rubbed him down to get the worst of the water off his coat and put a horse rug on him. The exhausted rescuers could only wait and hope the vet arrived before the young animal collapsed and gave up the struggle for his life.

Despite the heavy traffic, both the vet and the horse box arrived quickly and the vet set about administering lifesaving injections and getting fluids into this brave little horse. He was so weak, he could barely stand and it took the Police, the Horse Warden, the Vet and the driver of the horse box all their physical strength to get the little horse up the ramp and into the safety of the horse box. He was so exhausted, he showed no fear of being pushed and pulled up the small ramp. He would be well cared for now, with regular, small amounts of food being fed to him, so as not to upset his empty stomach. He was a world away from being out of danger, but his recovery would start now.

The horse warden went with the little Welsh Cobb to help settle him in his stable with clean bedding and access to badly needed food and water. A few days later, when it seemed he was on the road to recovery, The City Horse Warden asked the National Equine Welfare Council (NEWC) to put out a plea and her words, were as follows:

"On Tuesday evening, I received a phone call from the Police about a dead horse on the side of a road. As I approached, I realised the horse

was not dead, but very weak. I called a vet and we managed to get this little chap up. The vet then gave him the once over and said his vitals were ok, he was very underweight, but we would be able to travel him. He is now in a secure location and seems to be picking up every day. He is a little bay colt, probably last year's foal, very friendly, halter broken and leads very well. He picks up his feet and you can touch him all over. He has a lovely nature and because of his fighting spirit, I would really like to give him a chance. I understand everywhere is very full, but I do appreciate you taking the time to read this."

Roland, the owner of the Devon Horse and Pony Sanctuary at Manaton, Devon, read this plea and immediately arranged for poor little Humphrey (as we later named him) to be transported down to us. Roland wanted very much to make up for the dreadful things that had been inflicted on Humphrey in his short life. Roland then rang Sian, our yard manager at the sanctuary and asked her to prepare a clean stable for him, with a bedding of fresh chippings, water and hay. He told her that Humphrey was to be given very small amounts of food "little and often."

Sian rang me to tell me about Humphrey's impending arrival and sad circumstances. It tore at our heart strings to hear about his miserable start in life and his close shave with death. If that lady had not taken the trouble to stop and check on him, we felt sure he would have died and decided he must be made of stern stuff to survive as long as he did. We knew Humphrey would not be passed on to us unless he showed signs of physical recovery, so we were very excited at the prospect of helping to nurse him back to health, watching him grow stronger each day and into a large adult horse.

Humphrey arrived at our sanctuary on the morning of 6th March 2015. Bryan, a friend of Sian's, was on hand to help her unload him from the horse box, which the Cardiff Horse Warden had kindly provided for the journey from Wales. Sian was bracing herself for a very lively, if not nervous horse to emerge from the box. However, when the door to the trailer was opened, Humphrey stood with head bowed and was very quiet and more subdued than she felt he should be, but she put this down to the terrible ordeal he had just been through.

Humphrey had a thick, long, dark brown coat and his mane

was also dark brown, with a lighter brown colour running through it. He had a large white blaze running down the front of his face, which was matched by the white 'socks' on his legs and his feet were very large. His coat, tail and mane were so badly matted it looked as if it was going to be impossible to groom him. He was a very sorry sight.

Sian fell instantly in love with this forlorn creature. Already in her mind, she was picturing him when he was in better condition and she couldn't wait to see what he looked like as he grew and flourished.

As it was a sunny day when he arrived, Humphrey was gently led into our small top paddock, usually reserved for poorly horses. He immediately stuck his head in a feed bowl, and munched his way through that. When he had finished, he then tucked in to a small amount of hay, while Sian set to work trying to groom his dark, tangled coat. His reaction to this and all the fuss she made of him was quiet acceptance and he did not appear to be afraid.

Sian and her beloved Humphrey, taken a few days after his arrival.

Over the next few days, while his stable was mucked out, Humphrey was returned to the small paddock by the stables for an hour or two, to get some sun on him. Robin, our old blind Exmoor/Shetland pony was put in with him for a bit of company. Sian chose Robin, as she knew he would not show any aggression towards Humphrey. I found myself going up to the sanctuary on additional days to see Humphrey. I too, was quickly smitten and keen to form a bond with this quiet little animal.

Everyone who came into contact with Humphrey loved him and he certainly had a steady stream of visitors – Sian's friends, my friends and partner. He was so cuddly, not nervous or skittish like some young horses his age, which Sian estimated to be around seven months when he arrived. However, as the days went by, he continued to be subdued, which sent off a few warning bells in our minds. We felt that he should by now be showing a bit more of his personality and perhaps be a little mischievous. However, we continued to be convinced it was his terrible start in life which influenced his quiet behaviour.

Whether in his stable or outside he was very approachable and was being groomed several times a day by his adoring fans. Despite Humphrey's terrible start in life, he bonded with Sian very quickly, as she was with him six days a week. He perked up considerably every time he saw her, giving her a welcoming whinny each morning she arrived at the sanctuary. She always made straight for his stable before doing anything else, to give him a cuddle.

Each day, she would post pictures of him on our Sanctuary Facebook page and his story appeared on our Web page as well, generating yet more fans. Feeding him little and often gradually brought some of his strength back and after a week, Sian and her three year old daughter, Lola, were taking him for gentle walks through the country lanes, hoping this would cheer him up as he continued to be unusually subdued.

Our hopes of seeing little Humphrey getting stronger, looking better and being less depressed were sadly short lived.

Less than a month after his arrival, Sian arrived at the sanctuary one day to find Little Humphrey laying down in his stable. Whilst it is not unusual for horses to lay down in their stable, she was very alarmed when he did not get up straight away. It took her a lot of physical effort and patience but she eventually managed to get him to his feet and to eat his feed. A few days later she wrote in the Sanctuary diary: "Little Humphrey is not right. Vet called out." I joined her at the sanctuary that day to see Humphrey and to give Sian some moral support while Kevin, our vet was there. I knew how much she loved and cared for Humphrey and she was beside herself with worry.

Kevin took some blood samples and brave Humphrey stood calmly for him while Kevin administered Buscopan, (which suppresses spasms of the digestive system), Electrolytes and Glucose, via a tube up through Humphrey's nose and down his throat. Kevin's initial findings were worse than we expected. Poor Humphrey had "system shock, due to previous worm damage" and Kevin said that he was "struggling to cope."

The results of the bloods were back the next day and the prognosis was not good. The good news was there was no liver damage, but there was plenty of very bad news. Past worm infestation meant there were holes in Humphreys' gut, so the protein plasmas in his food that he badly needed for his immune system, together with the goodness in his food, were escaping and being wasted.

Kevin recommended we added a small handful of foal nuts to his feed to try and top up what he was losing from his gut. However, he warned us that any changes or increases in Humphreys' food must be gradual. The diagnosis explained why Humphrey had not put on much, if any weight and remained subdued.

Sian's feelings for little Humphrey had grown so strong, she came to dread going up to the sanctuary, in case he was laying down in his stable, or worse, dead. Her journey there was filled with foreboding so by the time she reached the village of Manaton, she started to feel sick at what she might find on arrival.

She decided to enlist the help of Julie and Bryan, friends of hers, for a bit of moral support. They had a lot of experience with and knowledge of horses. They agreed to accompany her each day to the sanctuary in case she needed help if Humphrey was found to be laying down. Although Humphrey was quite small and not at the weight he should have been, he was too heavy for one person to try and get him up on all fours. Bryan's job each morning was to get out of the car first and go over and look in Humphreys stable. If Bryan came back to the car with a 'thumbs up' and a large grin, Sian knew her beloved Humphrey was ok. Anything else and she braced herself for seeing him laying down in his stable.

I too started to dread going up there on my Wednesdays and was glad to have my friend Karen with me, for my own moral support. This support was going to be very important in those coming weeks, along with the physical strength needed to try and lift Humphrey up or roll him over.

Over the next week, most mornings Sian arrived to find Humphrey laying down, but the majority of these times, she managed to get him up. Some days, he even managed to get up on his own. Each time, he stayed on his feet for the whole time she was at the sanctuary. Did this mean he was getting better? We were on an emotional roller-coaster. One day he appeared to be fighting back, the next, his will to live seemed to be ebbing away.

We started to add milk pellets, (a feed that combines concentrated energy and protein milk with a complete vitamin and mineral supplement), glucose and feed balancer to Humphrey's food and in addition to this, Sian was giving him wormer. However, Kevin had to be called out again for Humphrey four days after we started these supplements. This time, the little horse was given a multi-vitamin injection.

I wrote in our diary that "Humphreys' eyes look empty." I was concerned that he might be blind, as he didn't appear to be looking at anything. Kevin said that he wasn't blind, he was giving up. His terrible start in life seemed to be weighing him down heavily and nothing we did could put a spark back into his eyes. Sian commented the next day that "Humphrey was not his usual self, head down."

A few days later, Sian was mortified to find that Humphrey's face was swollen, so she immediately called our vet out gain and Kevin took more blood samples. Sadly, Humphrey's condition continued to deteriorate. Although the swelling to his face went down a little, the next day, Sian found him non-alert and laying down again in the stable. Kevin was called out yet again.

Bryan and Julie helped Sian get Humphrey to his feet, but he was very un-stable and between the three of them, they were only able to hold him up for ten minutes. Then, he was gently lowered to the floor, on to a bed of fresh shavings and hay, with some old horse rugs propping him up. That was to be the very last time Humphrey was able to stand. We were not able to get him up from then on. Sian returned to the sanctuary later that day with a heavy heart, to check on him and this was the first of many evening visits.

Despite this set back, we all refused to give up hope and prayed our brave little Humphrey would show signs of some improvement. We were doing everything the vet had recommended and he was almost getting round the clock care. However, as much as we might imagine he improved slightly, it was not to be and with a heavy heart, a few days later, Sian called Kevin out once again. We all watched as Kevin tubed some Glucose through his nose and gave him yet another multi-vitamin jab.

Before he left, the vet spoke the words we had all been dreading. If Humphrey did not show any signs of improvement within the next few days, it would be kinder to put him to sleep. Given Humphrey's decline, we had expected this, but we were still hoping for a miracle. We were broken hearted and I avoided looking at the desolation in Sian's eyes.

All that was left for us to do, was to roll Humphrey over regularly each day, to try and reduce the danger of pressure sores. During the following days, brave little Humphrey ate all his food and some hay, with his head propped up in Sian's lap, as she held his feed bowl for him. I could hardly bear to watch him slipping away before our eyes, the will to live was leaving him at an alarming rate now.

Despite his failing health, Humphrey still called out a welcoming whinny to Sian when she arrived at the sanctuary each morning and evening. He adored her, the only good thing in his little short life. I was going up most days now, to do the feeds for the other horses and associated chores, so Sian could spend all her time with her beloved Humphrey. It was pitiful to watch the two of them together.

We were all pouring our love into him and giving him lots of cuddles, but we knew in our hearts now, that he was not going to get better. We were all torn between wanting to keep trying different remedies and continuing to call Kevin out, but wanting him free of suffering. His terrible start in life had made him give up. I think all of us knew he was going to leave us within the next few days.

Somewhere in the middle of all this, Sian hit on the idea of bringing Robin and Lucky in to the stable next to Humphrey, so he would have company day and night. It did not appear to make any difference to poor Humphrey, but at least it got the two oldies in out of the cold. Unfortunately, during this time, Sian arrived to find Lucky laying down one morning and had to call the vet out to him. Kevin diagnosed the horse had had enough – he was tired and very old. We were to find out later that having Lucky put to sleep, in full view of Humphrey, was to add to his depression.

Sian's days at the sanctuary were growing longer and longer. She was there from about nine thirty in the morning, to six at night and before she left Humphrey, she made sure he was propped up with bales of shavings, horse blankets and hay, praying he would be alive when she arrived the next day. I am convinced that if she did not have her three year old daughter to look after, she would have slept in the stable with him.

Sometimes on arrival, Sian thought Humphrey was alert, although still "flat out" in his stable. She was also trying some herbal seeds in his feed, which were supposed to fill the holes in his guts. Although sceptical about this, our vet said that this stage, anything we could give him might help and could certainly do no harm.

Poor Humphrey's mane and coat were becoming sweaty and matted, despite frequent rolling. We were all torn. Even at this late stage, we all knew in our heart of hearts he was going to have to be put to sleep, but although we did not want him to suffer, we were desperate to see if all the potions he was on, both natural and those given by Kevin, might turn him around.

I am not sure what broke my heart the most. Seeing this little horse giving up before our very eyes, or looking at the vain hope in Sian's eyes and watching her denial, as she cradled his head in her lap and spoke to him gently.

Still, we continued to feed him and syringe water into his mouth when he could not drink properly. He was still eating well, but now had a sore patch by his eye, from lying on one side, so now he had to have ointment on that as well. It was heart rending to cradle this little horse's head in my lap, my whole being screamed out that we should let him go. By this time the rest of us were gently telling Sian that she had to come to terms with the fact she would have to let Humphrey go.

In a last ditch and very desperate attempt to improve his condition, Kevin gave Humphrey Protexin (Protexin is designed to settle a foal's disrupted gut and helps in times of stress, change, antibiotic therapy or worming) and Sian reported that after this, she saw Humphrey moving his legs a lot and he appeared to become very alert.

Full of hope now, Sian continued to turn him, groom him and put drops in his eyes and Vaseline on his pressure sores. Kevin said since administering the Protexin, he had seen a very small improvement in Humphrey, which was the first time he had given us positive news since the start of his treatment. We all latched on to this and our hopes soared.

Unfortunately, the next day, Sian arrived at the sanctuary to find Humphrey had not eaten all of his food, but she continued to encourage him to eat by holding his bowl for him and giving him plenty of hay and water.

Desperate times call for what some people might call desperate measures and all of us were at the stage now where we would try anything to make Humphrey better. Julie knew a lady called Karen, who is a very successful horse whisperer, who lives locally. She calls what she does 'Touch 2 Talk 2 Heal' and has a Facebook page, with stories of her patients. More about Karen in Fie's chapter. Julie invited Karen to come and see Humphrey, with a view to finding out from him, if there was anything else we could do.

Julie recalls that Karen spent about an hour 'talking' with Humphrey and he revealed that he was very depressed. He told her his mother died when he was very young and her body was thrown into an old trailer by her gypsy owners. When he tried to get into the trailer to be with her dead body, he was thrown out of it and abandoned. He was missing her terribly.

In addition, he 'told' Karen that the reason he was laying down, was because if he stood up his stomach hurt. Although he was thankful and grateful for all the love and help we had given him, he didn't feel he could trust any humans again and couldn't find it in himself to try and look forward to a new life with us. He was too depressed at the death of his mother and his abandonment. He desperately wanted to be with his mum in heaven.

Apparently, seeing Lucky being put to sleep in the stable next to him was the final straw for Humphrey. He 'told' Karen that it brought back memories of his dead mother and looking back, we recalled that it was shortly after this, poor Humphrey's decline accelerated.

On a slightly jovial note, Humphrey showed a sense of humour. I mentioned earlier in this chapter that when Humphrey first arrived, we put Robin, our old blind horse in with him in the small top paddock. Following Lucky's euthanasia, Sian kept Robin in the stable next to Humphrey, for company. Humphrey told Karen that he found Robin "boring, as he doesn't say much" and said he would like some music in his stable because Robin was such poor company.

Sian's hopes for the continued improvement in little Humphrey's condition, following the administration of the Protexin were short lived, as he deteriorated again dramatically. Deep down, we knew our time with him was coming to an end, despite Kevin's fantastic efforts. Sian arranged for Kevin to come out and examine Humphrey the next day and we knew he would be putting our beloved little horse to sleep.

On the day Kevin was due, we all woke that morning with sick feelings in our stomachs, unable to eat breakfast. It was with a sense of terrible dread and very heavy hearts that the four of us all dragged ourselves up to the sanctuary that day. We all knew that poor little Humphrey would be put out of his misery and to be honest, as much as we loved him, we had all accepted he was not going to get better and didn't want him to suffer any longer. However, putting him to sleep after everything Kevin had done for him and all the love and care we had lavished on him, was absolutely gutting.

I arrived at the Sanctuary a few minutes ahead of Sian, Bryan and Julie. I headed straight to little Humphrey's stable, went in and cradled his head in my arms. I was crying and when Bryan came to peer over the stable door, although I didn't know him that well, I was out and into his arms, sobbing my heart out, unable to stop. Seeing Humphrey so ill and knowing we were going to lose him within the next few hours was unbearable.

We gave Sian some private time with Humphrey so she could say her goodbyes to the little horse she loved and adored so much. If pure love could have cured him, he would have been fit and healthy that day. The pair of them were exhausted with their respective efforts, him to eat and her to keep him alive.

When Kevin arrived, Sian and I were still in the stable, cuddling Humphrey. As Kevin examined Humphrey, no words were spoken. There was no need. One look on Kevin's stern face told us our worst fears were about to be realised. As Kevin knelt over Humphrey's ravaged body and filled up the syringe with the blue euthanasia liquid, Sian and I began to stroke Humphrey's head and our tears flowed freely.

The last thing brave little Humphrey saw as he slipped away, was his beloved Sian. "Has he gone?" she whispered. Our eyes were overwhelmed with tears and fixed on the vet's face. The grief was palpable within the confines of the small stable. Kevin touched Humphreys' open, sightless eyes very briefly with one finger and then checked for a pulse. "Yes", he said, unable to look at either of us, having told us the words we never, ever wanted to hear. I put my arm round Sian and hugged her as we both sobbed loudly.

Humphrey was barely eight months old and would have grown into a beautiful horse. Now he was lying dead, the warmth seeping out of him on to the stable floor. Neglect in his early months had finally caught up with him, despite all our best efforts. Perhaps in passing, he would be re-united with the mother he had been so cruelly separated from....

Prior to coming to our sanctuary, his little short life was filled with pain and misery. At least in the short time he spent with us, he knew what it was like to have plenty of food, water, warmth, shelter, care and lots of love. Despite all the horrible things which he had to endure prior to coming to us, we had found him gentle and affectionate.

I wanted to have a permanent, daily reminder of Humphrey, so I bought a rose just after he was put to sleep, planted it in my garden and called it Humphrey. Each year it bears lovely orange blooms and keeps Humphrey's memory alive each day.

Shortly after his death, I was at the sanctuary when something strange happened. It was a calm, sunny day, not a breath of wind. I was talking to Karen, when suddenly a carrier bag I was about to pick up from the floor suddenly rose up in to the air. It then fluttered down and swept along the floor, stopping outside Humphreys stable. Then without warning, it shot high up in the air to a point where it could not be seen. I am convinced to this day it was little Humphrey sending me a sign that he was ok.

The owners of our sanctuary posted the following on the Devon Horse and Pony Sanctuary Web page, following Humphrey's death:

Rainbow Bridge – Edited for Horses.

Just this side of heaven, is a place called Rainbow Bridge.

When a horse dies that has been especially close to someone here, that pet goes to Rainbow Bridge. There are meadows and hills for all of our special friends, so they can run with the wind and enjoy the companionship of their own kind.

There is plenty of food, water and sunshine and our friends are warm and comfortable; fear and worry free. All of the horses who had been ill and old are restored to health and the vigour of youth. Those who were abused, hurt or maimed are made whole and strong again, just as we would want to remember them in our dreams of days and times gone by.

The horses are happy and content, except for one small thing, they miss someone very special to them, who had to be left behind, so long ago. In each mind, there is a 'someone' who was kind, gentle and loving. One someone who took the extra step, stayed the extra minute, reached out and touched with love, even once.

They all run and play together, but the day comes when one suddenly stops and looks into the distance. His bright eyes are intent, his body quivers. Suddenly, he begins to run from the group, galloping over the green grass, his legs carrying him faster and faster. You have been spotted and when you and your special friend finally meet, you cling together in joyous reunion, never to be parted again. The happy nickering rings in your ears and a velvet muzzle nuzzles your face, your hands again caress the beloved head and you look once more into the big, trusting eyes of your special love and partner, so long gone from your life but never absent from your heart.

Then you cross the Rainbow Bridge together.

Author Unknown

COMIC AND COPPERFIELD: INSEPARABLE.

The Sanctuary was contacted in 2005 by a lady living in Bovey Tracey, Devon, who wanted to find a home for her horse Comic. She had owned Comic for many years and kept him in a livery yard on the moors. He was a thoroughbred, born on 30th June, 1995. His father was called Negro and his mother, Pidgeon Express. He was dark brown in colour and had a black mane and tail. She and her son had enjoyed riding Comic across Dartmoor. He was quite a ride, strong, fast and being a full thoroughbred he was a little unpredictable, but both of them were very good riders.

However, as time went by and the owner got older, her eyesight began to fail her. At this time, Comic was in his prime and was raring to go, but she began to lose confidence and felt unsafe whilst riding out on the moor. She couldn't see the ground properly to avoid the ruts and gorse bushes and she struggled to hold him back when he wanted his head. Comic was too exuberant to care, tearing across the moors at full throttle, enjoying every moment.

This was not the sort of horse that we would normally have offered a home to at the sanctuary, but his owner told the sanctuary owners that recently Comic had stumbled during a ride and ripped the muscles in one of his back legs. As a result, he had to have a large operation and his owner received an even larger veterinary hospital bill. Although Comic had recovered very well after his treatment, his owner was worried that this injury could re-occur and because of this he couldn't be sold as a riding horse.

Roland, Alison and their daughter Laura went to see him. He looked miserable and very depressed, so they agreed to take him, on the condition that his owner agreed to help a little with his everyday costs. She agreed to this, but after a while she could not sustain this financial outlay, as her husband developed Alzheimer's and she needed extra money to pay for a home help for him.

Comic arrived at the Hillside sanctuary in 2006. He looked magnificent, but like all new arrivals to the sanctuary, he was very wary. He had been bred, born and subsequently lived for all of his eleven years at the livery yard, so he was understandably nervous on arrival at his new home. He was put into a stable next to a horse named Copperfield, who had arrived a few weeks earlier.

Copperfield was a lighter shade of brown than Comic, with a massive white blaze down his face and long white 'socks' which came up past his knees. He was fourteen, a huge Clydesdale who had come to the sanctuary via an entirely different route. Clydesdale[4] horses are a breed of draught horses, derived from the farm horses of Lanarkshire. Characteristically, they are a bay colour with white 'socks'. The breed was originally used in farming and for hauling carts, and the Budweiser Clydesdales are a famous example of their original use. The British Household Cavalry also use these horses as drum horses.

He was one of a pair of trusty horses who pulled carriages in the grounds of the National Trust at Arlington Court in North Devon. These carriages were used to transport visitors around the grounds of the estate and up to the house. Unfortunately during the course of his duties in the summer of 2006, Copperfield sustained a shoulder injury, so he had to be retired early at the age of fourteen.

Rosie, whose job it was to look after the horses at the National Trust, had been put in charge of trying to find him a retirement home, but as he was such a big horse who had never been broken in for riding, she faced a very difficult job. Eventually, after contacting many other sanctuaries and horse charities who were not interested in giving Copperfield a home, she contacted the Devon Horse and Pony Sanctuary. Roland and Alison felt that as he was a Devon horse and had given his all, he deserved a safe and loving retirement home.

So, Sylvia, Alison, Roland, their daughter Laura and Ellie (one of the sanctuary helpers at the time) went to see Copperfield and enjoyed a day out meeting all the staff at Arlington Court. They were given a tour of the stables and carriage museum, which is one of the biggest in the country. All of them immediately fell in love with Copperfield and agreed to take him on. Unfortunately, the National Trust were not able

[4] Source - Wikipedia

to offer any form of financial support to the sanctuary.

The National Trust had been running a competition with other Trust properties to see who out of the male staff, had the best beard. Most of the men with beards were entered and so was Copperfield as his beard was quite magnificent. Copperfield won, so Rosie presented him with six bottles of best beer and took his picture so that it could go into the National Trust's end of year reports. Needless to say it was Roland who enjoyed the beer.

Copperfield was transported to the green at Manaton and was walked the few miles up to the Hillside sanctuary. He was accompanied by Rosie and the sanctuary owners, who had arranged for friends and supporters to be at Hillside, to greet the new arrival. Rosie, who quite obviously loved her charge very much, was very emotional about leaving him, but thankful that Copperfield had found a loving, caring home for the rest of his life.

Copperfield immediately found his feet at the sanctuary and settled in very well. Sylvia, commented that: "He has a big head, a big body, short legs and a HUGE appetite." Comic and Copperfield were paired up that May and immediately a bond was formed between them. Comic was the boss, but later developed separation issues with Copperfield and as a result, they became inseparable.

Shortly after Copperfield's arrival, a local newspaper asked Sylvia if they had any new additions they could report on. When they heard about Copperfield a photo shoot was set up in the yard. Roland had the bright idea of arranging for Copperfield to be surrounded by the amounts of food that he would consume in just one week.

So a huge sack of carrots, bales of hay and sacks of horse food were stacked up around Copperfield. Unfortunately, the photographer took so long setting up his camera and taking pictures of the sanctuary, that Copperfield had, by the time he was ready to start taking pictures of the horse, devoured half the carrots, eaten huge chunks of hay and tried to get into the bags of horse food. The impact of the shoot was lost.

Over the next few years, Copperfield remained a quiet and trustworthy horse and his shoulder injury did not cause him anymore trouble, he had not limped for two years. One day Roland thought it would be a good idea to take Copperfield into the nearby woods, to help him clear some of the paths. For a horse of his size, it would be very easy work and obviously something that he might enjoy doing. A harness was found for him, but when he saw the harness, Copperfield suddenly developed a very bad limp, so said harness was put away and never saw the light of day again. Did he imagine it, or did Roland hear a huge sigh of relief emerging from Copperfield…?

It was sometime later that Roland and the helpers at the sanctuary became aware that as their friendship had grown, Comic had developed anxiety and separation issues if he could not see Copperfield. Copperfield had become his whole reason for living. It was often remarked that Copperfield could live without Comic but no way could Comic live without Copperfield.

During Comic's time with us he suffered from a weeping and puffy right eye, which we bathed with an eye wash. In March 2011, our diary records that despite a gammy eye, Comic jumped a fence at Hillside. Shortly after this, both Copperfield and Comic were moved to Southcott, the other, larger sanctuary a few miles away.

Comic was quite an emotional horse. An entry in our diary states: "Comic getting sad, as Dolly appears to love Lewis more than him". Our horses do form emotional attachments to each other but these can be quite fickle. During this period, Dolly attached herself to Comic, often following him around and eating next to him. However, she also appeared to like the company of Lewis and maybe this was the reason Lewis and Comic were prone to the odd scrap. Both males and both basking in Dolly's admiration, they were found to be fighting on many occasions. Following one of these fights, Comic's back leg was swollen and a boot had to be put on to support his foot. A bandage was put on and the swelling went down quickly.

Comic continued to be in the wars during 2011. He suffered from a swelling in his throat, which the girls thought was a condition called 'grass glands'. The look of the Grass Glands[5] condition is similar to Strangles, but there the similarity stops. If a horse has been grazing for some time out in a paddock, they can

[5] Source – 'Holistic Horse' Web site

come in with a swollen throat and this swelling shows just behind the jawbone. These swellings are usually firm but painless and can be accompanied by fluid under the skin. Some think that these glands swell due to an allergic reaction to the grass.

Affected horses might look a bit like a hamster does when they store food in their cheeks. On most occasions, these swellings go down within three days, but if the swelling increases, the horse stops eating, gets a nasal discharge or becomes lethargic, it has to be seen by a vet. Thankfully, the girls' prognosis was correct, as Comic was soon back to normal.

A few months later, our vet was called out to stitch up a small wound on Comic. Kevin returned to take the stitches out during early August. Then in late August, Comic started to favour (rest) one of his back legs and became very jittery and the girls were unable to get a rug on him. The diagnosis was mud fever in his back heels. (See 'Cider's Chapter for details on mud fever.) As plans were being drawn up to move Comic to France, the girls were keeping his feathers (hair above his hooves) short, which reduced the effects of mud fever.

Copperfield was rarely in the wars, but in April, 2011 he got himself tangled up in some barbed wire, which resulted in cuts to his back legs. These were swabbed over and he was a little lame for a while. Unfortunately, this wire was already up when Sylvia bought Southcott. As the wire was only around the perimeter of the paddocks, the staff at the time felt the risks of the horses running into it were low. They based this risk assessment on the fact there had been no serious incidents involving barbed wire in all the years the horses had been at Southcott.

So, due to other priorities, financial and time constraints, we did not start to take it down until 2014.

There is only so much one person on their own can do. On a daily basis there is feeding, checking all the horses are injury free and have fresh water. Also, grooming, picking out their feet and giving the horses any necessary medication, mucking out stables and of course the back breaking poo picking. One of the girls could have organised a plan to take the wire down, but even if they could have rustled up the man power, this barbed wire could not be taken down unless alternative fencing was put up immediately afterwards. The supply and fitting of post and rail fencing costs thousands of pounds for just one paddock. It was money the charity simply couldn't afford.

In May of 2011, there is an amusing diary entry, which just goes to prove how dedicated the girls were who looked after the horses. Micala wrote: "Copperfield was weeing in a spray, so have cleaned his willy and lubed him up with Vaseline. Lovely job!!"

During the year between my starting at the sanctuary and Comic leaving to go to France, I had formed a strong attachment to my friendly giant. When I first saw him, I was over awed with the sheer size of him, however, I soon learnt that he was a very gentle horse. With his help, I graduated from practicing putting head collars on Robin, our little blind Shetland, to putting head collars on Comic. He was so large, he had to lower his head to enable me to do this. The girls also encouraged me to practice putting a rug on Comic as he was such a gentle horse and he seemed happy to oblige my clumsy attempts.

I had only been working at the Sanctuary a short time, when one of the girls found a puncture wound on Comic's chest. Initially, I was a little worried about applying the cream to this, but I soon learnt that he was an excellent patient. We never found out how he came to get this wound, although we inspected every inch of the perimeter fencing, we found nothing incriminating.

I was devastated when I was told Comic was going to France. He was one of the very few horses we had at that time, who gave me a great greeting on my arrival. However, I suspect it was because he knew I used to take Polos' up for him. Comic and Copperfield left for France on 21st October, 2011.

Now settled in Brantome, they shared a very large stable because Comic had to be able to see Copperfield at all times, otherwise he became anxious and stressed when his separation fears arose. Roland reports that moving to France calmed Comic down, but he did start to develop eye infections in 2012 and was treated by the vet in France, for a condition called Moon Blindness[6].

This is a chronic, painful, eye disease, and it's the most

---

[6] Source – 'The Horse' Web site.

common cause of blindness in horses. It was given this name during the 1600s by people who thought recurring attacks were related to phases of the moon. It is thought this eye disease might be one of the first veterinary diseases ever documented. Apparently, there are depictions of eye problems in cavalry horses of that time in the pyramids of Gaza, Egypt.

There have been many theories over the years as to what causes Moon Blindness. Some owners thought the condition was hereditary, some thought it was caused by damp, some said it was marshy pastures, damp stables or bad feed. Some even blamed town sewage for this condition, when farm fields with horses in them were irrigated with it. Modern theories are that it is caused by a lack of Riboflavin (Vitamin B) in the horses' diet or it is a bacterial infection.

Anyway, whatever the causes, unfortunately, despite the vet's efforts and Roland's best care, Comic eventually went blind in one eye, but for now, the other one is working perfectly. Fortunately, the vet managed to save the affected eye – normally they have to be removed. Comic is fine and happy, but Roland and his staff have to be careful when approaching Comic on his blind side, so he is not startled. Comic's previous owner, who used to visit him at our Sanctuary in Devon, still visits him occasionally in France.

In May 2014, Roland nearly lost both Comic and Copperfield. Roland had just taken a big bag of Sugar Beet (a dry food which needs to be mixed with water and soaked for 24 hours before given to the horses) out of a large feed bin and was about to open it and mix it with water, when he heard one of his volunteers calling out to him for help. He shut the door of the food store, left the stables and went outside to see what the volunteer wanted. Copperfield seized his opportunity for a meal (Roland said that even by horsey standards, Copperfield is incredibly greedy and although not their biggest horse, he is their biggest eater) and not only broke out of his and Comic's stable by very cleverly undoing the bolt on his stable door, but broke into the feed store as well and this was to have devastating, near fatal consequences for both horses.

Copperfield, with Comic eagerly following behind his beloved mate, immediately ripped open the bag of sugar beet

Comic and Copperfield at the Brantome Police Horse Sanctuary in France, being led in for their evening feed by Roland, the owner of our Devon Sanctuary and Brantome.

and started to eat. Sugar beet is super hydrated, which means that on hitting the back of the horses' throats and mixing with their saliva, the Sugar beet immediately turned into a concrete like consistency. Horses cannot vomit, so Copperfield and Comic had this stuff stuck in the back of their throats and couldn't breathe. They panicked and the noise of feed bins being knocked over alerted Roland, who rushed into the stable area. Ten minutes had gone by since Copperfield had ripped open the bag, but fortunately in that time, Comic had only managed to push his way in and grab a few mouthfuls, so he was not badly affected. Roland shouted desperately for help.

He could see the bulge in Copperfield's throat and frantically started to rub the area to try and break up the mass. He hoped this might get some of it down into Copperfield's stomach. In the meantime, Alison had come running into the stables and was immediately despatched straight back into the house to ring the vet.

Roland, his daughter Debbie, her husband Chris and a volunteer were now struggling to keep this massive horse on his feet. If he was allowed to go down on the floor, they knew he would die. Luckily, their French vet arrived very quickly and immediately stuffed a tube down Copperfield's throat to create an airway. He then attached a vacuum pump to this, to evacuate the swollen feed as the horse was very weak with the effort of struggling to breathe and looked as if he was not far from death.

During this struggle, Roland, Alison, Debbie, Chris and the volunteer all had their feet badly bruised as a panicked Copperfield kept standing on them.

Despite the pain they were all in, for four hours, the five of them frantically fought Copperfield's efforts to lie down. The vet refused to give up on this massive horse and was eventually able to stabilise him, once all the clumps of sugar beet had been evacuated from his throat and he was breathing freely. Copperfield and Comic were ushered into a trailer, to make the two hour journey to the veterinary hospital. Comic had to go, because, although he was nowhere near as bad as Copperfield, it was important to have him checked over. Just as importantly, he could not be separated from his beloved mate, because otherwise he would have become even more distressed and panicked.

The two horses were kept at the veterinary hospital for over a week during which time Copperfield developed an infection in his lungs. This was due to the fact some of the sugar beet had been drawn down into his lungs and he couldn't expel it. It was a very worrying time for Roland and Alison as they anxiously awaited for news of the two horses.

Roland said he has never seen a horse so glad to be going home when he went to pick up Copperfield and Comic nearly two weeks later. Copperfield was so delighted when he saw Roland and the trailer, he could not be restrained and galloped straight into it.

This was to prove a very costly accident, but both horses came through and valuable lessons were learnt from it. Now, no feed is left out of the food bins, which Houdini himself could not get into. Comic and Copperfield became two of the biggest attractions at Brantome Police Horses in France.

I always visit Roland and Alison when we are over in France

on holiday. I am not sure whether Comic remembers me, but it is always so good to see him again and to be able to give him a cuddle and some of his favourite treats, Polo's.

Sadly, Copperfield passed away just as I was finishing this book. He had just eaten two feeds and some volunteers at Brantome had given him a long groom in the yard before putting him back in his stable. Then suddenly he went down. The vet was called immediately and they managed to get him up with some biscuits and get him out in the field. When the vet arrived, he said that Copperfield's heart was giving up. Roland and Alison had a very hard decision to make.

So, with many tears and lots of long hugs, everyone said their goodbyes to Copperfield. Comic, his friend and constant companion for twelve years, laid down beside him as Copperfield quietly and peacefully slipped away. Comic was heard to be calling for his best mate and galloping round his paddock late into the night, looking for him. He is bereft and inconsolable. Roland has put Mikey and Matthew in with him to try and fill the huge gap in his life and help him over what will be a very, very long mourning period.

LEWIS AND JOY: SHOW JUMPING HORSES RESCUED FROM DEATH WHEN THEIR OWNERS NO LONGER WANTED THEM.

In early 2010, Debbie was contacted by a vet in the Suffolk borders. This vet had been asked to euthanize two healthy professional show jumpers, whose only crime was to reach the end of their working days and be of no further use to their owners. The vet was reluctant to destroy the two magnificent, healthy animals and asked the owners if they would be prepared to let her try and find these two horses good homes. The owners reluctantly agreed, but only gave the vet three days to do this. This vet contacted hundreds of charities and sanctuaries, but the Devon Horse and Pony Sanctuary was the only one to answer her with a "yes".

The vet even paid the transportation charges to transport them down to our Devon sanctuary. As soon as these two healthy beasts were on their way to Devon, their old stables were immediately filled with new younger models. No prizes for guessing what happened to these new horses, when they too were no longer of use to their owners. Let's hope not all race horse owners are this callous.

Lewis and Joy arrived at our Devon sanctuary on a Friday. It became quickly apparent that Joy, the older of the two, at nineteen, was of a different nature to Lewis. She was much calmer and able to cope with change. She was a lovely horse with a quiet nature and just wanted to please.

Following about a year with us, in 2011, Debbie managed to find her a wonderful foster home, where she was loved and cossetted until the end of her days in 2014.

Lewis was quite a different story. He was sixteen and had been used for speed jumping on the International circuit. Speed jumping is where horses jump against the clock and the higher the fences they clear, the more points they get. He was very successful and had earned a lot of money for his owners. But his life, like the majority of International show jumpers, had consisted of living in his stable, being taken out and exercised in a training ring before being put back into his stable, or being put on a transporter and taken across Europe to jumping events. He never knew what it was like to be a normal horse. He may never have been loved, nor had the opportunity to enjoy prolonged periods of being in a field, grazing in the sun.

As a result of this un-natural life style he was very highly strung.

On his arrival at our sanctuary, he was turned out to grass and paired up with Comic and Dolly for a little while, to get him used to being in a paddock with other horses. He was brought in every day so he still felt he had a set routine. It quickly became apparent that due to his previous solitary life, he didn't know how to socialise in his new peer group. Our diary records that on one occasion, Lewis and Comic had to be separated, as Lewis was attacking Comic.

For some reason, a few days after this incident, one of the girls put Comic, Lewis and Vera out in the same field together. The diary entry for that day, unsurprisingly, notes that there was a 'major fight' between Comic and Lewis, Lewis had attacked Comic again. Comic needed a lot of attention to multiple cuts and after that incident he was petrified of Lewis. Those two were never allowed in the same paddock again. However, Lewis must have been trying to get to Comic, as a few days later, the diary shows a warning in capital letters: "WATCH LEWIS, HE WILL TRY AND GET IN THE PADDOCK WHERE COMIC IS AND HAVE A GO AT HIM!"

During April 2011, when the girls had time, Lewis was regularly walked around the lanes surrounding our sanctuary, to the village green at Manaton. Although he was now receiving more attention, there are other recorded incidents which showed Lewis was still being destructive and aggressive in his efforts to reach horses in other paddocks. He knocked down part of a stone wall in his own paddock and the girls thought it was to try and get to Vera, as he had apparently become obsessed with her. This obsession manifested itself in many different ways. During one of our farriers' visits to the sanctuary during the second week in May, 2011, Vera was brought up into the yard so Lewis could see her whilst his feet were being trimmed, to stop him playing up.

Micala started to ride Lewis during this period, but reported to the other girls that she had problems getting him out of the paddock, due to his obsession with Vera. She found Lewis was, most of the time, difficult to handle as reared up for most of the duration of the rides. He was marginally better when ridden out with another horse, but was still prone to rearing up suddenly and with buttock-clenching regularity.

She took the decision to take Lewis back to her home in early June that year, on trial. She wanted to see if he responded to one-to-one care and if he became easier to ride. She knew Lewis craved individual attention and hoped to give him a permanent home. However, he became unhappy away from the sanctuary, so she took the difficult decision to move him back to his friends there within two weeks. She wrote in the diary: "Had last ditch attempt to ride him, with a friend on foot. Got round, but with lots of rearing and whipping round. Someone will crack him, but it won't be me."

Whilst Micala was disappointed to return him, Lewis was very excited to be back with his friends Vera and Gilly. Gilly is an ex-police horse who was with us for a short while before he was transported to Roland's sanctuary in France for retired Police horses – you will read Gilly's story in this book.

By now, the girls realised that Lewis was one very troubled horse and it would take a lot of care and devotion to make him happy. Although they lavished lots of love and attention on him, he was never contented as he had taken a shine to Debbie and he was only really happy in Debbie's company. However, Debbie lived in Bristol at that time and was not at the sanctuary regularly.

However, on hearing that Lewis still had not settled fully with us, Debbie decided to move him to a livery yard in Somerset, which was close to her home. She could see him every day, look after him and give him the love and individual attention he so very desperately craved.

When Debbie and her husband Chris made the decision to join her parents at their sanctuary for retired British Police horses in France, Lewis had to be moved back to the Devon sanctuary. He was only with us for the briefest of periods, because a lady called Jane, who lived in France and knew Alison, had asked if she could give Lewis a permanent home. Alison knew Jane was very experienced in rehabilitating horses with backgrounds like Lewis and was delighted that after being moved around a few times since Roland had agreed to give him a home, he would finally be able to settle down and get the one to one attention he still so badly craved.

Lewis was duly transported over to the sanctuary in France and this part of his life was all filmed for television by Channel 4, for the programme 'Little Britain'. This programme is about British people who have made a new life in the Dordogne. The filming of the preparation for Lewis's journey and arrival in France is covered in a later chapter in this book 'Channel 4 arrives'. Jane was there to meet him off the lorry when he arrived in Brantome, France and that was the start of a love affair which lasted for two years.

Jane was a very experienced horse woman and Lewis settled in straight away at his new home. Jane was able to give him the one-to-one care that he craved. He integrated easily into her herd and even got himself a girlfriend. Lewis was a very special horse, fully deserving the two years he spent with her, which must have been like being in horsey heaven.

Unfortunately it was not to last, as Jane decided after a few years, that she wanted to go on a world tour in a motor home. Poor Lewis was once again up rooted, but not back to Devon. He returned to Roland's sanctuary at Brantome and lived a happy life with lots of love and attention from his beloved Debbie, Roland and his family.

Due to the demands of his lifestyle before joining the Sanctuary, Lewis's body was on borrowed time. His kidneys stopped working, due to liver failure and as a result, he passed suddenly, but peacefully, in July 2014, with Debbie and her husband Chris by his side. Debbie, Roland and Alison were devastated when he died, but took comfort in the fact that although he had a very hard life as an international show jumper, his last years were exactly how he wanted to live and he was very, very happy. They were pleased that he had those four extra years during which he was loved and cared for.

When we are watching professional show jumpers on the television, we do not see, nor think about the lifestyle these horses have to endure behind the scenes, during their working life. I would like to think that not all owners are like those of Lewis and Joy. I hope the majority of these owners ensure their horses' lives have a good balance of travelling/jumping and time in fields or paddocks with their fellow jumpers, allowing them to 'be horses'. I would also like to think that then when these horses are past their best and can no longer earn their owners money, the more reputable amongst these people do their best to find them good homes, or are able to care for them into their old age.

CHANNEL FOUR ARRIVES AT THE SANCTUARY.

In the summer of 2012, Debbie rang me to tell me Channel 4 were coming to our sanctuary to do some filming, for the series 'Little England'. She asked if I wanted to come up on the day. Would I mind helping with and being involved in the filming? Be on the telly? Are you serious? What day and time did she want me up there?! I was very excited on two counts, one that I might be on national television and secondly it was a great opportunity to publicise our sanctuary. Maybe some donations would come in as a result of the filming. For those of you who haven't heard of the programme, it was about people from England, who have moved to the Dordogne in France, to start a business.

You will have read in an earlier chapter that Roland and Alison moved there in 2007 and settled in Brantome to set up a sanctuary for retired British Police horses. 'Lucky's story' includes the history of why Roland and Alison set up the Sanctuary in France.

The star of this Chanel 4 programme was to be Lewis, an ex-show jumper (You will have already read more details about Lewis in the previous chapter 'Lewis and Joy'). He was being moved over to France where the climate was much better than that on Dartmoor, because his health was deteriorating. It is not unusual for some of our Devon horses who have health issues, to be taken to France, usually because they will benefit from the warmer climate.

Lewis had not settled well in our Devon sanctuary. He craved individual love and attention and although we all make sure we give each horse a lot of love and attention, some horses need more human interaction; such as being ridden and to be able to attach themselves to one person. Lewis was going to France, as Roland had found him 'that person'. This lady was very experienced with horses and was also very excited to be giving Lewis a new home.

I was told Channel 4 wanted to do an end-to-end piece about Lewis, which would involve them filming us at the Devon sanctuary preparing Lewis for the journey. This would include them filming the vet carrying out his final checks, our grooming and rugging him up and walking him to the transporter lorry in Manaton, his loading up and our goodbyes. The film crew would then fly over to the sanctuary in Brantome, France and film his arrival there. Finally, they would end his story by filming him meeting his new owner.

On the day Channel 4 arrived, we were very lucky with the weather. It was sunny and warm. Sian could not be at the sanctuary so it was just me, Debbie and her two year old twins. I was up there bright and early in my new jacket (well, I was going to be on the telly) and polished boots – all ready for my debut on national TV. When the film crew arrived they told us how they wanted the day to pan out and the first thing they wanted to film was Debbie and I leading Lewis up from the bottom paddock. She had bought him a new blue and red halter and lead reign and as we led him up both of us were hoping he acted as good as he looked and didn't play up because of the camera crew and their equipment.

Some of our horses get paranoid and very nervous at any change in their daily routine. They knew they were normally only brought up to the yard when the farrier visited, or if they were poorly and needed to be stabled and seen by the vet. Therefore, when Lewis saw many people up there he didn't know, he immediately went on red alert, wondering what on earth was going on. He was a very large horse, so he would not have been easy to control if he had decided to take off during the time we were leading him up to the yard from his paddock.

Thankfully, he was very well behaved while the crew filmed Debbie and I leading him up to the yard and while our vet Kevin checked him over and issued his passport. They also filmed Debbie grooming him.

When Debbie had to disappear to sort out the toilet needs of her girls, she asked me to hold Lewis. I was pleased to do so but was then horrified when one of the camera men shouldered his camera and made his way over to me. As he shoved it into my face he said: "Would you mind saying a few words, love? I only want to ask you a few questions about the horse and how you came to be a volunteer here".

When I had told my friend and fellow volunteer Karen, about Channel Four coming up, she said: "For goodness sake, do not say anything to camera." She knew how excitable I was and how I rambled on. She did not want me to look foolish.

As soon as the camera was pointed at me, her words echoed around my head and my mind went a complete blank (no change there). Lewis' history disappeared from my mind as fast as melting snow and I couldn't for the life of me remember how long I had been working at the sanctuary. Needless to say that bit of filming, which probably only lasted a few minutes, never aired and is probably on the cutting room floor somewhere in a tin labelled 'interview with an idiot.'

To my immense relief, Debbie soon returned and took over. Now it was time to walk Lewis down the two miles of lanes which lead to the village of Manaton, where the transporter awaited us. The lanes leading up from the village are barely large enough to get a car down them and the transporters are so massive, it is customary for these transporters to wait at the village green at Manaton and we walk the horses down to them.

I got the job of leading this massive horse to the waiting transporter. Debbie drove her car very quietly and steadily in front, in case Lewis decided to play up, or worse, made a break for it – if necessary, she would be on hand to help. The camera man was in front, filming Lewis and I. Our fifteen minute walk was cut to a few seconds of film on the programme and you had to be quick to see it was me.

Saying goodbye to one of our horses just before they are lead on to the transporter is a very emotional experience for me. I knew I wouldn't see him again, unless I went over to France on holiday. I also worry the horse might not survive the journey. In addition, it is not pleasant seeing the horses tense and become very nervous when they spot the transporter. We know they are going to a great place, but they don't and I find it frustrating there is no way of letting them know there is nothing to worry about.

Being suddenly wrenched away from a place where you feel safe and the people you know cannot be easy for a horse, but Lewis continued to be calm as the back of the lorry was opened and his compartment was prepared. Debbie and I hoped this would give us a chance to say our goodbyes to this magnificent, but unhappy horse, but too soon, he was led away and into the back of the transporter. Both of us were struggling to hold back the tears as the doors closed and the tail gate of the lorry slowly lifted up. I found myself crying and hugging Debbie. To my horror, the camera man was over in a flash, sensing a good bit of emotional filming. He squatted down in front of us, his camera pointing up into our screwed up faces.

My appearance on national television lasted around two minutes, which, after a whole days filming was quite disappointing. I was shown with Debbie as we were leading Lewis up the field to the yard, filmed leading him down the lane towards the transporter and finally, my claim to fame came to an abrupt end after they showed me crying by the transporter.

This was quite embarrassing, because once we knew when Channel 4 were going to air that episode of 'Little England', I rang pretty much everyone I knew, telling them very excitedly I was going to be on national TV. I told them when it was on and asked them to watch the programme. It did not occur to me at the time that I might not be on at all, but even though my friends probably blinked and missed my appearance, at least a few minutes air time was better than nothing.

The episode made very good viewing, as the viewers saw Lewis being readied at our sanctuary, his departure from Devon then his arrival at Roland's sanctuary in France. The filming ended with a short clip of him with his new owner, Jane.

RUDOLPH, SNOWFLAKE AND CRACKER: ALSO RESCUED FROM DRIFT SALES.

These three ponies were saved by Roland from the drift sales in Tavistock in 2008. The earlier chapter on 'Freddie, Boris and Heathcliff' has information on these drift sales. A friend and benefactor of the Sanctuary for many years had rung Roland and asked him to attend the drift sales and buy two ponies on her behalf. She wanted to ensure that at least two could be saved. Roland contacted the BBC, who said that they would be interested in making a film for the television programme Animal 24/7, so, accompanied by a couple of friends, Roland attended the sales with a film crew.

The livestock pens consist of heavy steel enclosures with concrete floors and clanging metal gates. The wild ponies are herded down ramps from transporters into the pens. Very few of these frightened animals have had any contact with humans. They immediately go to the corners of the pen all trying to hide in the centre of the group, with the foals trying to find their mothers. It is an awfully sad sight to see.

One by one, they are chased into the sale ring, where they are met by a cacophony of noise and they are surrounded by people. The auctioneer, shouting from a loud speaker, tries to get the best price for each one and their future is then decided. Roland and Alison looked at all the ponies in the pens, agonising over which two to buy. It was heart wrenchingly difficult as all the ponies needed their help, but the sanctuary did not have the resources to take them all.

Roland decided on two Dartmoor ponies which were painfully thin and very nervous (Rudolph and Snowflake as they later became known.) He also looked into a larger pen and saw four miniature Shetland ponies. One was a mare with foal and she also appeared to be pregnant again. There was a bigger black foal which appeared to be coping and another very tiny brown and white bedraggled foal. It was obvious this little foal was very young, as he was trying to suckle from the pregnant mare. He was desperately missing his own mum and he was so exhausted he found it hard to stand and tried to lean against

Snowflake and Rudolph at the drift sales

Cracker

There were two hundred and twenty three ponies for Roland to choose from.

her but as he was not her foal, she kept pushing him away.

The little foal was one of the last to be put into the ring. He was alone as all of his companions had been sold to a dealer. He was exhausted, bewildered and very frightened. Roland felt he deserved a safe and secure home and he managed to buy him for the price of a few packets of cigarettes. He named him Cracker.

The other ponies and Cracker had already had a long and terrifying day, but they still had the long journey from the drift sales in Tavistock, to the Sanctuary in Devon to get through. They all huddled together for comfort in the back of the large horse box, during the journey back to the Sanctuary at Hillside.

In preparation for their arrival, Walter, a huge Police horse, had to give up his stable for the night until Roland and Alison could get the new horses stables organised. Walter was bemused at the sight of his small sad looking lodgers, but the new arrivals soon cheered up when they were given as much food as they could eat and a few treats.

A bemused Walter peering in at his guests.

Eden meeting Cracker for the first time.

Cracker's first few months of life were filmed and shown on the BBC 1 programme Animal 24/7. He had such a sweet nature and even the most nervous person around horses couldn't be frightened of him. When Cracker arrived at our Devon sanctuary, another pony called Freddie took him under his wing and they became inseparable.

In April 2012, Roland and Alison had to bring Freddie to their sanctuary in France, as Freddie was suffering badly from bouts of Laminitis. Cracker had to go with him as they were so close. He lives to this day at their sanctuary in Brantome. Both ponies are spoilt and Cracker continues to work with children and adults who may benefit from close contact with an animal that they can spend time with and love.

As for Rudolph and Snowflake, Roland hoped that once at the Devon sanctuary, he would be able to arrange for them to be broken in, to enable him to turn them into little riding ponies, so they could then be put out on loan. Rudolph and Snowflake were not broken in, as the charity could not afford the cost, but they were loaned out to a lady who lived in the nearby village of Manaton. She did not want them as riding ponies, but just to keep the grass down in her paddocks.

Some years later, in the summer of 2012, I was asked to move Rudolph and Snowflake, who were by then fully grown adults, from our other sanctuary at Hillside, where they had been living since they were returned by the lady who lived in Manaton. I was to walk them over to our main sanctuary at Southcott. Karen was with me that day and although she had not been working with us for very long at that time and had no prior experience with horses, she was well up for the challenge. I was very worried that with two horses to manage and a nervous, if not plucky novice helping, there was all sorts which could go wrong. Whilst Hillside was only a few miles from our other Sanctuary at Southcott, the lanes between were very narrow and there were quite a few cottages along the way, most with barking dogs on guard, alert to any stranger passing by. Spook potential for two nervous horses.

Despite the fact these two horses were not broken in, they allowed me to put head collars on them. I did not know Rudolph or Snowflake very well and had no idea how they might react to a car squeezing past us, or a dog hurling itself at a gate barking loudly. If that was not worrying enough, we also had a village to negotiate and a cross-roads to get past. I had only worked at the sanctuary for a year, but I knew that even our smallest pony had a lot of strength, so it was with great in trepidation that we began that small journey.

I needn't have worried as we met no cars or stroppy dogs and the two horses were very well behaved. Karen was a natural and very confident in the end and we managed to walk them both over with no incidents. When we arrived at Southcott, we put them into a paddock with Bramble, but the initial interaction between them was not good at all. Bramble is a large horse and did not take very kindly to his new companions.

I was reluctant to move Bramble into another paddock, because I didn't know why he had been moved into the one the new ponies were going in. Despite my frequent requests to the girls, asking them to write in the diary why horses were moved, nothing had been written in the diary on this occasion either. I rang Micaela immediately and told her I had moved Bramble and asked her to come over and check on them later. I also re-iterated my request for them to keep the diary up dated when horses were moved.

By June 2014, we were walking Rudolph and Snowflake around the paddocks and lanes outside the sanctuary, to get them used to being handled, to give them more interaction with us and to get them used to having head collars on.

Over the coming few years, Roland made various enquiries as to the cost of having these two broken in. However, all the people he approached with the skills to do this were charging between £800 and £1,000 pounds per horse. As we are a charity, Roland was not comfortable spending such a large sum of money, when so much is needed to run both the sanctuary in France and our Devon Sanctuary.

When Micala returned to the sanctuary, in October 2018, on top of making sure all horses were handled regularly, she and her friend and new member of staff Joy, decided to try and break Rudolph and Snowflake in themselves. They could see that both horses had good natures and would benefit from being ridden. Within a few months, both horses were being ridden and Joy has ridden Snowflake out around the lanes near the sanctuary.

The first time Rudolph has Micala on his back.

Micala on Snowflake for the first time.
Wez, her husband is leading.

GALLIPOLI: ROLAND'S 24 HOUR DEADLINE TO SAVE HIS LIFE.

Gallipoli was born in 1998 and had devoted seven years of his life, on front line duty, in the Metropolitan Mounted Police Force. He had been an exemplary horse during this time, but suddenly started to buck and either take off at speed with his rider, or throw them off completely. He got to the stage where he wouldn't even tolerate a saddle on him, so the Police decided to have him checked out by their vet.

He was diagnosed with 'Kissing Spine Disease'[7], which occurs when the bony spikes at the top or sides of the vertebrae start to rub together. In some cases, it causes pain and swelling, especially when the horse is moving. Not all horses suffer pain from this condition, which makes it difficult to diagnose. Poor Gilly was then deemed 'un-rideable', so the Police decided he had to be put to sleep, as he was no longer any use to them.

Lucky for Gilly, during the week of his diagnosis and subsequent death sentence, the boss of the Metropolitan Police Mounted Branch was visiting Roland's sanctuary in France. He was there to see how the other ex-Metropolitan Police horses had settled into their new life overseas. He told Roland about Gilly and asked him if he would consider taking him on. However, Roland was given only twenty-four hours to agree to take him, otherwise Gilly would be put down that week. Of course he agreed immediately – another life saved.

Gilly's passport just says "horse", so Roland has no idea what breed he is, but thinks he is an Irish Draft cross thoroughbred, or a thoroughbred crossed with Warm blood[8]. The word thoroughbred is sometimes used to describe a breed of purebred horses. These horses are known for their agility, spirit and speed and are bred for specific purposes, such as racing, polo and show jumping to name a few. Warmbloods are a result of cross breeding Thoroughbreds with other breeds.

---

[7] Wikipedia

[8] Warm blood, thoroughbred and Irish Draft information source - Wikipedia

The term Warmblood describes horses classed as middle weights and this distinguishes them from heavy draft horses (called 'cold bloods') and the more refined lighter horses, such as Arabs (called 'hot bloods'.)

The Irish Draught horse is, of course, the national breed of Ireland and these were initially bred to be an all-round working horse, ideal for pulling loads in harness and for riding and farm use. Today, it is popular to cross these with Thoroughbreds and Warmbloods, to produce high quality sport horses. The pure bred Irish Drafts are popular as Police mounts because of their temperament and strength.

In May 2011, Gilly was loaded into a huge Metropolitan Police horse transporter in London, to begin his long journey down to our sanctuary in Devon. Here, he would be rested for a while, getting acclimatised to being in fields and running with other horses, until we felt he was ready to be transported to Roland's sanctuary in Brantome, France.

By now, the locals at Manaton had become used to seeing the massive transporters arrive but some villagers still come out and lean over their gates to watch the proceedings. As the transporter usually blocks access to the road around the green, passing traffic cannot get through for a few minutes, so motorists often watch as our new arrivals are lead down the ramp.

The day Gilly arrived was no exception and villagers watched as he began his walk along the few miles through country lanes to our Southcott sanctuary. His walk was un-eventful, as you might expect, because dogs rushing up to gates barking furiously or cars speeding round the small lanes did not phase this ex-Police horse. On arrival at the sanctuary, he was stabled in sight of other horses and calmed down quite quickly, when he realised he was not on his own. The girls had debated where to put him. It is always a bit tricky deciding which paddock to put a new horse in, because we do not know the nature of the new horse and who he might mix with well.

Initially, the girls chanced putting him in with Lewis, our ex-show jumper, but although Gilly and Lewis got on well at first, Lewis became edgy and aggressive around Gilly when Vera was in season. A diary entry for that week screams: "KEEP ELECTRIC FENCING ON!" Within a few weeks, Gilly was happy to be

Gilly

brushed and have his feet picked out and is reported as being a "real gent, very calm and still." He accepted and adapted to his retirement and the easy, unregimented country life very quickly.

When I think about Gilly, I remember a massive but gentle horse. He was easy to handle. I was very sorry to see him go when he was deemed settled enough to be taken over to Roland's sanctuary in France, in September 2011.

On his arrival, the first thing Roland did, was to have Gilly checked over by his own vet. This vet concluded that he didn't think Gilly was in any pain due to the Kissing Spine Disease, so he did not recommend either surgery, or the more common treatment of a Corticosteroid injection. Gilly settled in excellently in France and continues, to this day, to lead a relaxed and very happy life with Roland and Alison's other ex-Police horses.

CAPTAIN AND HERBIE: LITTLE AND LARGE

Herbie, a little white miniature black spotted Shetland stallion, was rescued by the RSPCA when he was twenty years old. He was taken away from a cruel breeding stud, where the owner bred miniature spotted ponies. At the time the RSPCA raided this stud, there were dead and decomposing ponies just left lying around the site.

Herbie had received terrible injuries during stallion fighting. His last fight was with his own sire and he nearly lost his life during this vicious battle, which resulted in the death of his sire. The RSPCA vet immediately put Herbie into their intensive care area and he was on a drip for three weeks. The vet did not think Herbie would survive.

As Herbie's treatment progressed and he grew stronger, the RSPCA vet decided to geld him (horse equivalent of castrating a dog or cat) because it was felt it would give him the very best chance to be able to be re-homed, as this would calm him down. He came through the gelding remarkably well and was soon homed to a lady who wanted to take him on and give him a good life during his recovery process.

Herbie quickly settled into her field and was soon accepted by her two mares and geldings with no problems. Unfortunately, as this lady could only keep Herbie temporarily, once she felt he was fully recovered, she set about trying to find him a permanent retirement home - telling prospective owners he was quite shy with not an ounce of aggression.

Unfortunately, despite all her efforts, she could not find Herbie a permanent home. She approached Roland, who agreed to take Herbie, early in 2010, when he was twenty-five. Debbie, Roland's daughter, looked after him, lavishing a lot of love, care and attention on him. Following a period of recuperation and rehabilitation with Debbie, he went out on loan on 21st July, 2011 to a lady who lived in Bristol and needed a companion for her old horse 'Captain'.

Captain and Herbie made unlikely friends, as Herbie is very small, but with a very big opinion of himself. Captain was the biggest horse I ever saw, elderly, but distinguished and an elegant thoroughbred with impeccable manners. They quickly became inseparable and developed that very special bond that equines can sometimes establish. Sadly (there always seems to be a 'sadly' or 'unfortunately' in these horses' stories) Captains owner became very ill and was unable to look after them. She contacted the sanctuary and asked if Roland could not only take Herbie back, but also his big best friend. They arrived at our Devon sanctuary in October 2012.

The owners of our sanctuary had rung to ask me if I would meet the transporter, which was bringing Captain and Herbie down from Bristol, to the usual drop off point, in the village of Manaton. The only details I was given about these two, were that one of the horses, Captain, had 'separation issues' with his constant companion Herbie and at no time should he be out of sight of his mate.

When the ramp went down at the back of the transporter and Captain was led out, I was in total awe of the sheer size of him. I was very nervous about leading such a massive horse, who I didn't know at all, the one and a half miles from the village to his new home at Hillside. How big would the other one be? I didn't think I could I cope with both.

I held my breath, waiting for his best mate to emerge, expecting his companion to be equally huge but Herbie turned out to be a miniature spotted Shetland, barely bigger than my collie. I laughed with relief and was warmed by the sight of their reunion. It was comical to think that such a strapping horse like Captain couldn't bear to be separated from this tiny little horse.

I was also massively relieved when the staff of the equine transportation company said they would lead Captain up to Hillside, so I just had to manage Herbie. Considering the long journey from Bristol must have unsettled them both, they were very calm as we led them to their new home.

I had prepared their stable the previous day, so all was ready for them. Lots of fresh chippings, hay nets hung up and a big container of fresh water. I was asked to put a rug on this massive giant before I left them to get used to their new home. The rug itself was a lot bigger than my king size quilt, with loads of straps and Velcro and a neck piece. Nervous around a new horse – I had no idea about what other aversions/foibles he might have - it took me about five attempts to get this rug on the right way round and secured properly, but Captain was happy munching away on some feed and seemed very tolerant of my repeated attempts to rug him up.

Following a week which enabled them to get settled in at Hillside, two of the girls at the sanctuary walked Captain and Herbie the few miles back down to the village of Manaton and back up the other side to Southcott, our main sanctuary. Here, the paddocks were much bigger and more level. Captain and Herbie settled into their new paddock very well, enjoying the bigger space and their new, larger concrete shelter.

Horses seem to have their likes and dislikes of people, even though at the sanctuary, Sian and I treat them the same. Sian always maintained Captain didn't like her, although she was far more confident around him than I was. Whilst sometimes she couldn't get anywhere near him or catch him, I could pretty much do anything with him, including dabbing a swollen eye with the appropriate ointment, putting fly cream on him and I once rugged him up with two rugs, as he was shivering in the winter.

When the farrier came, it was me who caught him and led him up to the yard so his massive feet could be done. However, he would only tolerate the farrier if Herbie was there with him and Herbie was at that time, a little blighter to catch. It was a daunting task trying to hang onto Captain, as he didn't like the farrier mucking about with his feet, even with Herbie close by.

Whilst Captain was very approachable, Herbie was not. No one could catch him, which I found amusing, considering he was such a small horse. Giving him carrots was and still is a bit of a problem because he brings his head up, draws his lips back from his (large) teeth and lunges at your hand. We call him Suarez, after the ex-Liverpool player – who also had a reputation for using his prominent teeth.

On 23rd February 2014, Sian called our vet out to Captain as she suspected he had colic and she was right. Colic is a very serious condition. It kills thousands of horses every year. This condition is explained in more detail in Pippins' chapter. She transformed Captain's field shelter into a stable, by putting down some fresh chippings, hay and fresh water for him and also, somehow got his best mate Herbie in with him.

On her arrival the next day, she saw that Captain was not right and called Kevin out again. She quickly fed the other horses and then spent an agonising three hours waiting for the vet's arrival, with Captain's head cradled in her lap. Sadly, Kevin had to put Captain to sleep as he diagnosed a displaced large intestine. Captain slipped away peacefully, his massive head still held lovingly in Sian's arms. Our gentle giant was no more, but we took comfort in the fact he knew he was loved very much by all of us and his final years had been spent quietly and very happily with his best mate.

They covered his body over with several horse rugs, but as the crematorium lorry could not come until the next day, his body had to stay in that paddock overnight.

Captain looking over the hedge at me.
He was a huge, but gentle horse.

Whilst Captain was, hopefully, galloping over Rainbow Bridge, to join past friends, the worst was to come for us. On top of the grief and stress of watching a horse die, the next stage is almost as bad. The body has to be brought up to our yard. Brian Warne, our farmer neighbour, responded to our request for help and turned up in his tractor and dragged Captain's body up through several paddocks, to await the crematorium lorry. We do our best to ensure the body stays covered and receives respect, but unfortunately, there is no other way to get deceased horses up to the yard.

Whilst the cremation people do their best to get to us quickly, looking at the body of a dead horse even under blankets is something I will never get used to.

We now had to decide what to do with poor Herbie, Captain's constant companion. Sian moved him in with Vera, Haidi and Holly. Holly had recently been returned to us from being out on loan. She looks just like Herbie, very small and white but she has a few small grey markings on her rear. Herbie did not show any outward signs of grief at losing Captain and whilst he was not by any stretch top dog in his new paddock, he seemed happy enough.

Following the arrival and settling in of Peaches and Victor, they were also moved in with Herbie, Vera, Holly and Haidi and they all got on really well. A few months later, when Holly, Vera, Peaches and Victor, went out on loan Herbie and Haidi were left to share a paddock together and Herbie seemed unaffected by these changes.

All of us were growing concerned that although Herbie seemed happy enough, he had not been seen by our farrier for a while, because he was impossible to catch and repeated attempts only stressed him out. I was able to get close enough to him to give him a little back massage, but any attempts to try and get a head collar on him failed as he ran off as soon as he realised what was happening.

However, when Lara, one of our new permanent members of staff arrived to work with us at the Sanctuary, she made it her mission to befriend and catch Herbie. She was determined to get him to trust her and worked towards being able to run her hand over his sides and back. She managed to achieve this after only a few weeks, but Herbie was as dismissive of her attentions as he was with ours. He would walk off after a few minutes.

Lara arranged for a local horse trainer to come in and work with Herbie. Lara, Kelly (another new member of staff), me and Sian all worked under Anna's quiet but firm instructions as we gradually herded Herbie and his mate Haidi into their large concrete shelter. Amazingly, within less than ten minutes, Anna was able to stroke Herbie and massage his back. Within another ten minutes, she had a head collar on him and a few minutes after this, a lead rope.

Herbie was quiet and submitted to her gentle voice and hand commands and I could not believe how good he was. Lara continued to work with Herbie until she left the sanctuary a few months later, but the rest of us are continuing to handle Herbie and he now sees the farrier regularly. Herbie remains very partial to a nice back massage and although sometimes he is easier to catch than others, he continues to be caught on a daily basis and has responded well to this handling.

When Micala returned to our sanctuary, she continued the regular handling and as a result, Herbie had his first dental appointment, as we were concerned he had problems with his teeth. He was the perfect patient.

Herbie

DEIRDRE, TARA AND DAPHNE.

Early in 1996, a man called Heathcliff, who knew Sylvia and Terry, the owners of the sanctuary at that time, rang them to say he had rescued two mares off Bodmin Moor.

He told Sylvia both mares were in a terrible condition, malnourished, with hooves that had grown so long, they were barely able to walk. Heathcliff asked if Sylvia would keep them for a couple of days whilst he found them a home. Sylvia agreed, but unfortunately, after delivering these two ponies to her, he then disappeared. Although messages were passed through a mutual friend, he never returned for them. Sylvia had no choice but to keep them and she named them Daphne and Deidre.

Daphne was very elderly and they believed Deidre, a wild spotted grey pony was her daughter. Sylvia thought Deidre was in foal and she was correct, as Deidre's foal was born at midnight on the 28th May 1996. There were no problems during the birthing process, although the foal managed to fall in a horse trough within an hour of being born and Sylvia had to rush to his aid in the dark with just a torch and pull him out. She named the foal Dennis.

A few weeks later Daphne died of old age but although this brought sadness to Sylvia, she consoled herself with the fact Daphne had enjoyed her short stay and was in a much better condition than when she arrived, thanks to the care Sylvia had given her. She had spent the last few weeks of her life in a warm stable, with plenty of food, love and attention. When Dennis was weaned, Sylvia found him a home with one of her best friends and to this day, Dennis still lives with her.

During her time at the sanctuary, entries in our diary show that Deidre was difficult to approach and handle. The staff persevered and eventually managed to get a head collar on her and after many months of hard work and gentle coaching, got her into a stable.

Deidre was also very nervous of the farrier, so in preparation for his first attempt to do her feet, the decision was taken to sedate her. It is very important that horses' hooves are kept filed back, because if they grow too long, it affects the way a horse walks. However, when this was first attempted, the girls found she was not "dozy enough", so on that occasion, the exercise was unsuccessful. Her nervousness must have increased because the girls had to sedate her again, just to get a head collar on her again in late August 2011. This was in preparation for her going out on loan with another of the sanctuaries horses, Tara, in September 2011, to a family in Cornwall.

Deidre had attached herself to Tara and they became constant companions. Whilst it must be said that our staff at the sanctuary never gained the trust of Deidre, despite their dedication and hard work, they were delighted to hear that Deidre came on in leaps and bounds since going to live in her foster home with Tara. This is due to the one-to-one care and devotion her foster mum has given her.

Tara is a pure white Irish Draught / Connemara Cob[9], who had been bought by a lady who used to ride her regularly at a riding school. The Irish Draft and Connemara Cob breeds both originate in Ireland. The Draught horse was bred specifically for farm use, to be an all-round working horse. They were suitable for working in harness, pulling carts and being ridden. Today, they are crossed with Thoroughbreds and Warmbloods, which produce the popular Irish Sport Horses, which excel at the highest level of eventing and show jumping.

Connemara Cobs are known for their versatility, good nature and athleticism. Connemara, where these horses originate, has a very harsh landscape which has made these horses hardy with a strong disposition. Connemara's are known as sports ponies, being very versatile in show jumping, dressage and eventing. However, they are also used in harness and for endurance riding.

In April 2004, the lady who had bought Tara from the riding school suffered a marriage break up and she left her job at the stables, where she had been allowed to keep Tara. She hadn't been able to sell her as Tara was regularly on Bute, an anti-inflammatory / painkilling powder, due to lameness. Because of this no one wanted to take her on as she was classed as un-rideable.

In addition to the lameness, Tara had never liked being

---

[9] Source - Wikipedia

ridden. When she coughed a lot, the riding school rested her, so she learnt that if she kept coughing, she would not have to be ridden. You will have read a similar story of this intelligence and reasoning in Comic and Copperfield's chapter. Copperfield used to put on a 'limp' when he saw he was to pull a small cart of wood the owner had collected in the woods around the sanctuary.

Tara's owner contacted our sanctuary to find out if we could take her. When Roland and Alison arrived at the riding school to see Tara, she looked amazing, as her owner had given her a good clean and a really good groom. However, Roland and Alison immediately saw why Tara had a problem with lameness.

The field she was kept in was very steep, with no flat areas other than the one which had been cut out of the side of the hill specifically to put a shelter on. Tara was constantly having to adjust her considerable weight to compensate for being on the slant the whole time. They also saw she wasn't the friendliest of horses as she was determined to keep her distance from the two strangers. Despite all of this, Roland and Alison took the decision to offer her a home. They felt they could help her in many ways and wanted to get her out of that awful field as soon as possible.

She arrived at the Devon Horse and Pony Sanctuary a few days later. A lot of time and effort went into settling her in, making her welcome and determining the best horse to partner her with. As she had been on her own for the last few years, Roland and Alison and the staff at the sanctuary were worried about how she would react to company. Several horses were tried out, until she was put in with Deidre and they took to each other immediately. This was a huge improvement in Tara's life, company and a flat paddock.

Not long after Tara arrived, Alison saw that as Tara was an ex riding school horse, she was very quick on the uptake where food was concerned Tara would have been used to stiff competition in the fields to get to and eat food and it seemed to be her only reason for existing. One evening at the Hillside sanctuary, Alison had fed all the horses in the stables and was clearing and sweeping up when she could hear a lot of banging coming from Tara's stable. Looking over the stable door, Alison watched in amazement as Tara, having finished her dinner, picked up her yellow bucket and was banging it on the floor so that any food stuck to the sides fell into the bottom where she could finish it up. How clever she was!

When Tara had been at Hillside for about two years, her lameness had completely gone and she was no longer on Bute. Occasionally Alison would take her out for a ride across the moors, accompanied by Roland, riding Guardian, one of the ex-Police Horses at the sanctuary. On one occasion, whilst trying to put the saddle on Tara, Alison was amazed that the girth strap (the one that keeps the saddle on) would not fit. It turned out Tara had bloated her stomach out deliberately to stop Alison being able to get the girth done up. Both her and Roland tried for ages and then gave up.

The next day, Roland and Alison arrived at the sanctuary to attempt to ride out again. Despite their worries, they were delighted when Tara allowed the saddle to be put on her and walked over to the wall where Alison mounted her. Both Alison and Roland were starting to feel like they were actually going to make it out on to the moors and were in high spirits. However, as they set off up the drive which led out on to the road, Tara started to limp.

They felt they had no choice but to turn around and give up again. When they reached the yard, they removed her saddle and bridle and put her out in the field. They then stared in amazement when Tara galloped across her paddock, kicking up her heels and neighing without the slightest sign of a limp. Probably the horse equivalent of the 'up-yours finger'. That's when they both realised Tara had just had enough of being ridden and wanted retirement.

This horse, whose talents included putting on a cough, faking a limp, deliberately bloating out her stomach so she couldn't be saddled and banging her food bowl to get more food out, had cleverly engineered her well-deserved retirement. To this day, Tara and Deidre continue to live out their days very happily in their Cornish home.

PIPPIN: NO LONGER WANTED BY HIS FAMILY.

Pippin is a Dartmoor/Haflinger cross pony, born in 2001. The name 'Haflinger'[10], originates from the village of Hafling, which is in northern Italy. This breed was developed during the nineteenth century and today, this bloodline has been infused with various other breeds, such as Arabian and European breeds.

Prior to us taking him, Pippin had been bought and owned by a lady when she was in her late teens. She subsequently married and had two boys and thinking the boys would be interested in ponies, she allowed them access to him on a daily basis. However, as the boys grew older, they started to ill-treat Pippin by beating him with sticks, which resulted in poor Pippin leading a very unhappy existence.

Despite the fact she could see the horse was very stressed, the mother somehow came to the conclusion that the boys were "just playing" and amazingly allowed the situation to continue. Sometime later, she finally changed her mind, finally noticing her sons were making this horse's life a misery. She made the decision to try and find Pippin a new home. (Personally, I would have got rid of the kids, but that's just me.)

She contacted Roland, and asked if we could give Pippin a home. Hearing his story, Roland agreed immediately, but in the middle of making arrangements to have him moved to us, for some reason, she changed her mind and tried to find him a home elsewhere. Unfortunately, due to his stress levels brought about by the ill treatment Pippin had received at the hands of her children, she was unable to rehome him. Not surprisingly, as her boys had been so nasty to him, Pippin had become very difficult to catch, which resulted in him being classed as a 'naughty pony'.

The woman contacted Roland some time later and luckily for Pippin, Roland agreed to take him, work with him and then try to rehome him. Following a few years at our Southcott sanctuary in Devon and being treated as he should have been, with loving care, he had settled down really well and began to trust again. He became a very friendly horse and was reasonably easy to

[10] Wikipedia

catch. The owners of the Sanctuary took the decision to move him to their sanctuary in France, where they felt the climate might suit him better and they thought they had more chance of finding him a new permanent home with the right owners.

When Pippin had been at the French sanctuary a short while, a young French girl showed a keen interest in him and she used to come and ride him in the nearby woods. Pippin loved this, but unfortunately, her family would not allow her to keep him at their home. After a while she stopped coming and poor Pippin was left to wonder why.

Shortly after this, Roland found him a home with another young girl, whose parents had assured Roland both they and their daughter were very competent horse people. Whilst a thorough check is carried out before a horse is moved to a new home, this does not normally include stipulating that the new owner must show Roland they can ride. A short time later, during a home check, it became apparent very quickly that Pippin had not been ridden much, if at all. It turned out that none of the family were good riders. The owners admitted to Roland that their daughter was unable to ride Pippin, because he was too strong for her.

Although Pippin had a great temperament, he was too wilful for her as a first pony. He had also started his old trick of not wanting to be caught again, so after a year the family gave up on him and returned him to Roland's Brantome sanctuary.

Roland and Allison were very sad at this turn of events, because they were sure they had found Pippin his 'forever home'. All of us always feel we have let a horse down when they are returned to us, after we have sent them out on loan to what appears to be an excellent home, only to have them returned at a later stage. This is the unfortunate life of the horse, but better for them to be back with us, to be cared for properly.

Even after all my time at the sanctuary, I continue to be amazed at some of the reasons people give us when they return the horses.

Roland decided the best thing was to return Pippin to our sanctuary at Southcott to live out his days in peace and quiet as he did not always get on well with the Police horses at that sanctuary. Pippin arrived back at Southcott, on 11th October, 2012. Once again, the huge transporter lumbered into the sleepy village green at Manaton and Sian and I were there to meet Pippin, when the massive doors of the transporter opened and he was led down the ramp. I was in charge of walking him up the lanes to our sanctuary, with Sian following very slowly in her car. He appeared very quiet, probably traumatised by his long journey and, given his past, wondering where on earth he was going to end up and for how long.

Initially, we put Pippin in our largest paddock, with our little blind Shetland Robin, his mate Lucky and Cider. However, to our horror, Pippin started running around the paddock lashing out with his back legs at any horse who had the misfortune to be nearby. Poor old blind Robin took a kick and Pippin also took an instant dislike to Cider, so we immediately moved Pippin down with the mares.

The next day, Sian began her attempts to make friends with Pippin, to make it easier to catch him.

Pippin gradually settled down with his new herd, but remained a bit hit and miss when it came to trying to get near him to give him a cuddle or treats. Catching him for the farrier was also tricky. He was a very gentle, quiet horse and when he was stabled due to laminitis, he was very approachable and allowed us to groom him and make a lot of fuss of him. However, as soon as he was back in his paddock, he was back to being aloof and un-touchable.

Kelly, one of our two new members of staff, officially started with us on 6th April, 2017 and what a baptism of fire she had that day. She was to be trained by Sian who was teaching her the daily routine. On arrival they found Pippin sweating and Sian suspected Colic. A horse with suspected Colic is always treated as an emergency, so she called Kevin our vet out and he noted the sweating, increased breathing rate, lots of rolling and restlessness and confirmed her diagnosis of possible colic.

He administered a pain killer to relax him, in the hope that once he was calm, Pippin's gut would start to work properly. He advised Pippin should be stabled without food, only water and that Sian should come back and check on him later in the day.

When Kevin left, I think Sian rang Roland and there was a long debate as to whether Pippin should be stabled, as per the vet's advice, or allowed access to a small paddock so when he rolled around to try and get rid of the pain, he would not injure himself. There appears to be differing opinions as to the best option with Colic.

I understand that it was agreed he should be gently walked around to try and ease his pain before Sian left. What I am not sure about is whether he was left overnight in our small paddock, in front of the yard, with access to a stable, or whether Sian shut him in the stable. Sian said when she returned to the sanctuary later that day at 2:30 pm, there was "evidence of Pippin's rolling in the stable" and he was still very sweaty.

The vet was called again and he arrived at 4:30 pm. The diary shows Kevin did more tests on Pippin and said it would be a "waiting game" until the morning. Kevin admitted he did not expect Pippin to survive the night. Sian left the sanctuary at 5:30 pm. That would be the last time she saw Pippin alive. Pippin lost his battle with the pain of colic and passed in the night.

Lara, who was due at the sanctuary the next day, for her first day's training, was there first at 08:15. While she waited for Sian to arrive, she went to check on Pippin and saw he had died in the night. It was clear he had thrashed around a lot in the stable, judging by the amount of blood there. What a traumatic first day at the sanctuary is was for her as well.

He was dearly loved by all of us, so we were all devastated when he died. One day he was fine, the next, exhibiting all the signs of a horse with Colic[11]. Colic is a term used to describe abdominal pain and it can indicate a problem with internal organs within the abdomen or a problem with the gut.

Colic has many impacts, which can include indigestion at the bottom of the scale, right up to a twisted gut. Colic can be caused by many things: stress due to a change in routine or travelling, poor feeding regimes such as a lack of fibre, or a sudden change of diet and poor grass. It can also be caused by problems with teeth, as poorly chewed food increases the risk of clumps of food blocking the intestines and also gut damage. The list is long. Good horse management techniques can reduce, but not eliminate Colic.

If you look up 'Colic in horses' on the Internet, it will tell you

---

[11] Source – 'Blue Cross' Web site.

that Colic is common today, because horses eat a different diet from when they first evolved. Their natural feeding habits meant that the horse was on the move constantly, grazing whilst travelling. It is estimated that a horse used to spend around sixteen hours a day eating. Some horses today spend a lot of time in stables, with hard food and rationed hay – far removed from their ancestor's lifestyles. Even horses kept in large paddocks still lead different lives, compared to their ancestor's constant roaming, feeding as they go.

The result is that the modern horse's intestines have not evolved quickly enough to meet the changes and because of this, they are susceptible to digestive upsets. As I mentioned in Comic and Copperfield's chapter, horses cannot vomit, so they are unable to expel toxins or food they cannot digest. Therefore toxins are absorbed into the gut quickly.

The list for Colic prevention is also long. It includes fresh water, regular worming, and a diet of high fibre with hay forming sixty percent of the intake. If exercise, feeding regimes or any part of the horses daily routines need to be changed, these changes must be brought in slowly.

Regular dental checks should be carried out and spring grass should be rationed as it is very rich.

His paddock at Southcott looks empty without our gentle friend.

Pippin with his distinctive 'white saddle' mark.
Love him.

CIDER: THE ONE WHO LOVED SQUARE CRISPS AND CUSTARD CREAMS.

Cider arrived at our sanctuary in March 2012, with a letter from his owner. There was also a little note book from Becky, the lady who was his main carer, called 'Tips for looking after Cider'. There were fourteen pages of his likes, dislikes and information about him, from the time his owner acquired him at age twenty, in November 2010. Here are some of her notes:-

- He loves human food just as much as, if not more than his own. His favourite crisps are salt and vinegar squares and he loves custard creams.
- He likes it when you sing to him.
- He will do ANYTHING for a banana.
- Don't pay attention to his ears, look at his eyes, they tell you what he is thinking.
- Give him your heart and he will give you his.
- He acts as if he doesn't need anyone. This is NOT true.
- Cheap and effective homemade fly spray: 20 drops of tea tree oil, 20 drops of white thyme oil and 20 drops of lavender oil. Put these three things in 200 ml of water and put in a spray bottle. Shake before use. Can use on people and horses.
- He likes being talked to as if he is a baby or a child.

Cider was dark brown with a black mane and a small white blaze down his face. The first time I met him, he was standing cowed at the back of his new stable at our Hillside sanctuary. His ears were back and he would not come forward to meet me right away. It took me a good half hour of speaking to him gently before he eventually got his courage up to come forward in response to this coaxing. His ears remained flat back and his eyes were wide with fear. Not surprising really, when you think how a horse must feel, when he is suddenly taken from a home he has come to know and people he loved and trusted.

It was difficult to know where to put Cider. According to his notes, he did not like other horses much. Following a settling in period at our Hillside sanctuary, Sian walked him over to Southcott, which is our larger sanctuary. After a few days of trial and error, Sian was eventually able to settle him into a paddock with some mares – Shannon, Fie, Vera and Haidi. Cider now had a little herd and once he found his feet, he seemed comfortable with them. Vera (or vicious Vera, as we still call her) needed someone to keep her in check and Cider took on the role very well. She was no longer in charge of the small herd once Cider settled in.

Cider suffered terribly from sweet itch. In horses, ponies and donkeys, this is an allergic response to the saliva in the bite of the Culicoides midge which gives rise to intense itching. Due to his allergy, as soon as the warm weather comes each year, we put a 'fly' rug on him. This is a light rug, with a neck piece and a full face mask which also protected his ears. The more of his skin we could protect from the midge bites, the better. Once bitten, he was in pain afterwards as his skin would become raw. However, he regularly rubbed off the gauze over his ears and he had to be caught to rub cream on his broken skin.

He wasn't always easy to catch, even though we kept a head collar on him. Most of the time, he had to be bribed with food. This was very difficult because once the other horses saw we had food, they thundered over and crowded in, wanting their share. I think he got through two or three of the full anti-fly rugs in so many years. In the height of summer, if the flies and midges were too bad, we brought Cider in during the day. Flies, although partial to a bit of horse poo and horses skin, do not like the shade.

Cider did indeed have a passion for salt and vinegar square crisps and custard creams. These were only given on very rare occasions and in very small quantities. When he became injured on barbed wire and was stabled for a considerable length of time, these treats, in moderation, were used as a morale booster and to keep him still whilst his medication was administered over the months that followed.

As you will have read in a previous chapter, I first started helping at the sanctuary in June 2011. Following lengthy training and nearly the same amount of time being supervised, I was eventually trusted to go up there on my own, to feed and look after the horses. I felt honoured that I was trusted, but I always lived in fear of being the first and only person on the scene in the event of any injury or death.

My worst fears were realised a few weeks after 'going solo', when I arrived at the Sanctuary and saw Cider with blood pouring down his chest. The butterflies in my stomach became as large as birds. Feeling sick with apprehension and panic, I ran over to him and saw a large puncture wound on his chest, which was bleeding profusely. I rang Sian in a panic and she told me to put Hibiscrub on it. Hibiscrub is a liquid antiseptic skin preparation. It is designed to disinfect skin, helps to kill germs and is a general cleanser.

I ran back to the barn, where we kept the first aid cabinet and found some Hibiscrub in there. Not for the first time since arriving, I wondered why I couldn't have chosen painting or yoga to do in my spare time. What was wrong with gardening and lunches out? Heart thumping, I grabbed some cotton wool and headed back into the paddock.

I was very worried I might not be able to catch him and even more worried that once I caught him, would he let me treat the wound? These fears proved unfounded, because, as I was to learn over the years, when our horses get injured or fall ill, they seem to know you are going to help them. I caught him easily, and braced myself for his reaction as I poured the antiseptic liquid into the open wound. In my mind, he was going to rear up (I must have watched too many programmes about 'Fury', 'Black Beauty' and 'Trigger' in my childhood) try to kick me or at best, run off. To my surprise and immense relief, he didn't even flinch.

Sian called into the Sanctuary later in the day to check on him and decided our vet should come up and see him as soon as possible. Kevin's diagnosis was that Cider's wound was nasty and deep so he stitched it up and gave him anti-biotics. He also gave him penicillin and tetanus injections and flushed the wound out with saline and antiseptic. He told Sian the wound must be allowed to drain and must be flushed twice daily with a saline solution, via a plastic syringe, straight into the wound.

In addition to this, Cider had to have an injection of Duphapen Fort, which is used for the treatment and control of a wide range of local infections, twice daily into his rump. He was to be kept in a stable for five days, and have Bute (a pain killer in powder form) added to his food each day. We noted in the daily diary we kept, that if Cider was to go downhill, the vet should be called immediately.

Before I left that day, I inspected every inch of the perimeter fencing and gates in Cider's paddock but could find no clue as to what had caused this deep puncture wound. Sian also looked all round his paddock, in his shelter and in the hay feeder in the paddock but also drew a blank. To this day, we still have no idea what on earth could have caused this damage.

Poor old Cider accepted his daily treatment graciously and I continued to marvel at how a horse, not accustomed to being stabled or handled regularly was such a star to treat. If someone had squirted salt water into an open wound on me, I would have reacted violently, but this big horse just stood still and let us do it. It was a bit of a baptism of fire for me, which bolstered my confidence. Little did I know at the time, worse was yet to come.

Five days later, the vet was out again to check Cider's wound. Kevin told us that his wound still had to be flushed out daily and have penicillin gel in it once a day, but he could be let out into our small paddock. Cider was re-introduced to being outside, but only overnight at this stage – partly for his own safety and also because the lady in the house opposite the sanctuary was complaining about the noise Cider was making as he continued to kick the stable walls! Cider was very pleased with himself when he was let out, bucking his way around the paddock, so we concluded he was feeling much better.

For the next few weeks Cider's wound continued to ooze pus, (more custard anyone) which I found alarming but was told this was positive and the other good news was the amount of blood in the wound was decreasing.

However, his wound still needed to be squirted with a pint of salt water and we were still applying his penicillin paste and Hibiscrub. By the end of June, Cider was out all the time but proved to be hard to catch to continue to have his wound treated. By early July, Sian recorded in our diary that: "Cider's lost the plot today, doing the bucking thing around the paddock like he did in the stable, kicking fences and gates, wouldn't be surprised if this is how the wooden gate was off its hinges yesterday. Haven't been able to do his shoulder, but the wound looks clean."

Cider was stabled again a few weeks later, as he was kicked by another horse and his old wound was looking gunky again. It was becoming a struggle to keep this horse out of trouble. Sian was not sure if the gunk was the Citronella fly cream, or whether the wound was weeping, so she stopped applying the fly cream.

His stay in the stable was extended because it seemed the number of flies around were the worst Sian had seen for years. Each summer as we all battle to catch our horses and get them to stand still long enough for us to cover their faces in Citronella cream, I wonder why no one has been able to invent something to put on horses that can deter flies for longer than a few minutes. We have even tried the Citronella tabs which attach to head collars but the flies come back with a vengeance almost immediately after the application of the cream or putting the tabs on their head collars.

Cider was eventually turned out permanently, back to his normal paddock with his herd of mares with his fly rug on. He looked like a medieval horse in his gear. His joy at being back with his herd was fantastic to watch, lots of galloping around and calling. Now out of the confines of his stable and the small top paddock, he went back to being difficult to catch when we needed to put his ears back in his face fly mask.

Later that year, he was in the wars yet again with suspected mud fever in his right back hoof. I learnt that bacteria causes mud fever, as it lives in soil as spores and can survive from year to year. These spores become activated by wet weather and this is why we see the disease when the ground is wet.

Mud fever[12] is not limited to horses that spend a lot of time in mud. Mud fever can range from a mild skin irritation to very painful infected sores and can, in some cases, cause significant swelling with severe lameness. The condition affects the lower limb, most commonly the back of the pastern (ankle in human terms.) When the same condition occurs on the upper body it is referred to as 'rain scald' and in the cases I have seen, all the horses' hair comes out in clumps. It looks very alarming, but

---

[12] Source – staff at the sanctuary

soon grows back. It turned out that Cider did not have Mud Fever, but a worse event was to befall him four years later, early in 2014 when his previous bouts of trouble would pale into insignificance.

In the meantime, by mid-September, poor Cider continued to be in the wars once more. Early one morning, Micala found him lying down on her arrival. He was lame when he got up. Micala examined him and concluded laminitis was to blame and immediately moved him to our small top paddock, where there is not much grass. It was testament to the loving care he received, that by early October, he is reported as looking "fab."

On a Tuesday, in early January, 2014, Sian arrived at the sanctuary to start the feeds. The weather was awful, cold and raining very hard. As Cider was in one of our lower paddocks, it was a while before she found him lying on the floor, completely entangled in barbed wire. He was terrified, exhausted and bleeding badly from his efforts to free himself. She was momentarily locked in fear as she surveyed the poor horse.

She was in a quandary – she did not want to leave him, but her mobile was in the barn, two paddocks away. She had no choice but to leave him, if she wanted to try and save his life, as she needed to ring our vet. She was off at a hard run, uphill through two paddocks, thick with mud which made the going tough. Adrenaline spurred her on, as she prayed that Cider would still be alive when she returned. She could not bear the thought that he might think she had abandoned him in his hour of need.

Sian rang the vet first, then put in a panic call to her partner Carl, then to Julie and Bryan, his grandparents. They all dropped everything and rushed up to the sanctuary to help. Julie recounts that she "went hell for leather, to get there as fast as I could" but she was very worried that she wouldn't be able to find the Sanctuary, as she had only been there once before. Luckily, her memory served her well and she and Bryan were soon running across the muddy paddocks to join Sian, who was trying to keep the badly injured horse calm.

Carl arrived shortly afterwards. Ben, the son of Brian Warne, the farmer who lives opposite the sanctuary, also responded quickly to Sian's phone call for help, as did Roland's daughter who lives locally. All of them worked carefully but frantically in the next hour to free Cider from the barbed wire wrapped around his back legs and chest. During this time, Cider was calm and subdued.

They eventually managed to get him to his feet and Bryan led him up through the two paddocks to the stable, very, very slowly and gently. Looking at the wounds all over Cider's body and watching copious amounts of blood pour from these wounds, Sian thought it highly likely the vet would put him out of his misery straight away. She was very concerned about the severity of the cuts on his chest and back legs. Both the tendons and bones in his back leg were clearly visible.

By the time they got Cider up to a stable, Kevin, our vet was there. Despite the fact Ciders' injuries were extensive and his pain excruciating, he remained good natured during the vet's examination and treatment. Kevin said, to everyone's relief, that although Cider's wounds were terrible, he felt with the right care, he would recover, but it would take a lot of time.

It would be the responsibility of Sian and the rest of us, to bathe Cider's wounds daily with warm salt water and to change the bandages in between Kevin's visits. I am still in awe of how good Cider was during what must have been a very painful time for him.

In addition to the wounds on his body, there were deep cuts to his face and a few days later on the 11th January, we found another cut on his chest, which was only now visible because some of the swelling around it had gone down.

I was out of the country when Cider had this accident, but as soon as I returned home, I dashed up to see him and burst into tears when I saw the extent of his injuries. Roland and Alison, arrived just after me. Seeing the state I was in, they immediately assumed he was dead.

Kevin came out again on the 14th January to change Ciders' bandages and inspect his wounds. In our daily diary, the entry for the 17th January reads: "Cider very lovable." How amazing considering the pain he must have been in.

Kevin's weekly visits continued. The diary shows visits on the 21st and 31st January. On the 6th February, after sedating Cider, Kevin had to remove 'proud granulation' tissue from Cider's back leg. 'Granulation tissue' is vet's speak for brand new tissue

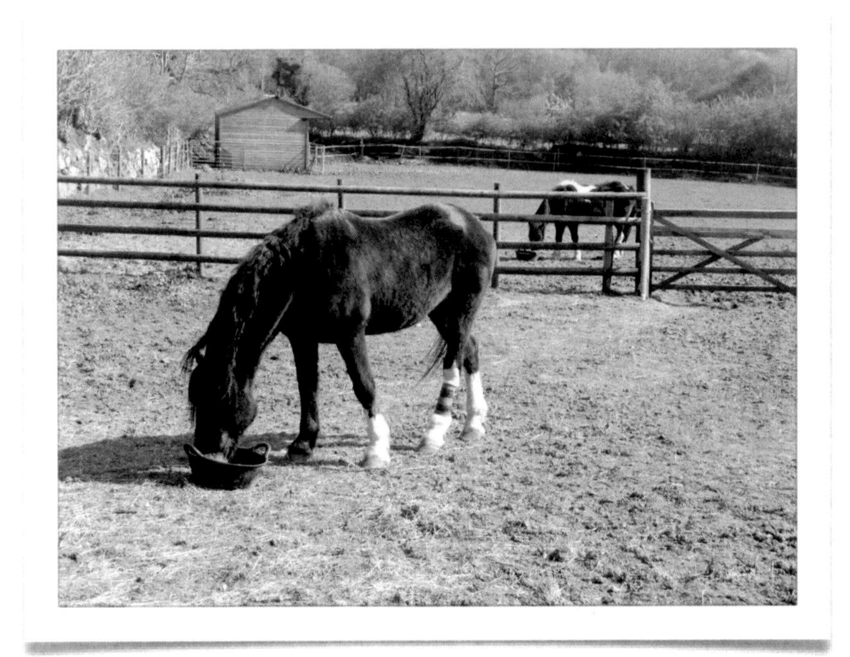

Cider recovering from his injuries in our top paddock, five months after his accident. (Pippin in background.)

growth. It was called proud, as it had grown so much, some had to be shaved off. There was a lot of blood, so even though I had gone up to the Sanctuary that day to see Cider and help Sian hold him while Kevin worked on him, I ended up outside the stable as I could not bear to watch and see all the blood. Some help I was. On his next visit, on the 10th February, Kevin was happy with the way Cider's leg was healing.

However, within a week of Kevin's last visit, Cider was favouring his bad leg, so once again, Kevin was called out to examine him. By the end of February, pus was seeping out from the top of Cider's bandage and running down his leg. I found this very alarming, but apparently, Kevin reported he was happy with Cider's progress during another visit to change the bandage a few days later.

On the 11th March, Kevin gave us the good news that he felt Cider could be seen every two weeks, instead of weekly. He was on the road to recovery! That day, Cider was let out into the 'yard', a small space between the top paddock and the stables which enabled him to move around freely but safely.

Cider eagerly awaits his custard creams.

This was the first time he had been out during the day since his accident in the first week in January. The first thing he did when he was let out of his stable, was to roll, then he trotted up and down the fencing, calling for his herd.

During this time, the sanctuary owners approved the purchase of more wooden posts and rails. Sian and Julie organised an army of helpers to take down the barbed wire where Cider had become entangled, replacing this with the wooden posts and rails. There was no way Cider would be allowed back in his paddock until every last piece of barbed wire was taken down.

Kevin's next recorded visits were on 8th, 15th and 29th April, to check on Ciders progress and to change his bandages. We were delighted to hear him say that: "Cider's leg looks incredible." On the 13th May, Ciders' dressings were replaced with Tubigrips (elastic bandages). On this visit, Kevin said: "He has a way to go, but he is going in the right direction."

By mid-May, Cider was moved from the small grassy yard, to a small paddock we reserved for poorly horses. During the first week of June, a member of the public reported us to SWEP (South West Equine Protection) because they saw the bandage on Ciders leg and stupidly assumed he had been ill treated by us. If I saw a horse in a sanctuary with a bandage on, I would assume it was receiving treatment for an injury. As a result of that, all our horses were inspected by SWEP and their findings were, as we expected, that our horses were being looked after excellently.

Six months after his accident, Cider was being left out over night and was resplendent in another new full fly rug and head gauze. On 10th July, Kevin came up to see Cider, to remove some more proud flesh from his back leg. Once again, Cider was an excellent patient. Credit must be given to Sian, who was changing Ciders' bandages weekly, often on her own.

Roland and Alison continued to fund the purchase of more posts and rails so we could take down barbed wire in other paddocks, making these areas safe and enabling us to segregate some of the larger paddocks. This also helped us to rest the grass and move the horses around. During August we had a 'fencing day' which Sian and Julie organised during which many people gave up their Saturday to work all day taking more barbed wire down and replacing this with posts and rails. We finished the day off with a BBQ.

It was an exhausted, hungry bunch who sat down much later in the afternoon to eat burgers and sausages in baps loaded with fried onions. Sian is an avid cake maker and had been busy baking the night before, so everyone could finish off with a bit of homemade cake with their cuppa.

We were all very tired, but happy that we had done a good job and hopefully prevented more accidents. I think all the horses loved the company as well and I am sure that Cider, who was stabled at the time, revelled in all the attention.

In November, 2014, eleven months after Cider's barbed wire incident and four months after his full recovery, Sian arrived one morning to find Cider laying down and in a lot of pain. She immediately rang Kevin, who diagnosed 'Displaced Intestine' (twisted gut). This is only cured by surgery and although Roland was prepared to pay to have this done, Kevin said Cider's age was against him and Cider was immediately put to sleep.

I cannot describe in words how devastated we all were. We had all played a part in his very long recovery and thought he would be around for a good many years to come. For me, I had grown to love this horse who had stood still for me when I squired salt water up into his chest wounds and treated and dressed (clumsily) the wounds on his back legs. A horse who had my respect for the fact he had been in so much pain but was never once aggressive with those of us who had to administer painful treatment.

We were all in a state of shock. Cider had been through so much, the puncture wound, laminitis, and severe sweet itch each summer. Then the terrible injuries when he was caught in the barbed wire. He had survived all that, but now he was dead. Dead! We could not believe it and it did not seem right. He had been so very brave but now he would not be with us anymore.

To make matters even worse, the local animal crematorium company could not send a lorry to pick up Cider's body until the next day. When the vet had gone, Sian tearfully covered Cider's body with old horse blankets as his lifeless body was a tough sight to see. Cider was Bryan's favourite horse and he was absolutely gutted. We were all broken hearted.

In the past, when the crematorium van arrives to collect one of our dead horses, we girls normally made ourselves scarce and Bryan would have the awful job of overseeing the horse's body being dragged up through the paddocks, into the crematorium's van. We couldn't face it.

When the van arrived to collect Cider's body, we all felt sick and Bryan found he could not face it this time. This was one dead horse Bryan could not watch being dragged into the crematorium lorry. Seeing his tears only added to our grief. Julie raced over to ask Brian, the farmer opposite, if he could help. Luckily, he said he would, so we all were able to make ourselves scarce.

Seeing a beautiful animal's dead body being dragged up through our paddocks and into the cremation lorry is not one I have ever been brave enough to watch. However, due to their size and weight, there is no other way to get them up through the lower paddocks, into the yard and into the lorry, so it is something we have to accept.

Cider's death was a very cruel blow to all of us and very difficult to come to terms with. He had survived his terrible injuries from the barbed wire and been the perfect patient for eleven months. I could not believe we had now lost him to this. Our only consolation, was that because of his confinement after the injuries he sustained in January of that year, he had enjoyed more human contact and love than he would have done, had he been with his girls in his paddock.

Julie made us bracelets out of some of Cider's mane and I wear mine all the time in his memory. Rest in peace, our brave boy.

LOUIS: EX-POLICE HORSE, OUR GENTLE GIANT.

This magnificent, huge, ex-Police horse arrived at our sanctuary on 23rd August, 2011. He was stunning to look at, chestnut in colour, with a black mane, a large white blaze down the front of his face and four matching white socks. His Police rider, as is the normal procedure, journeyed down with him from his stables at The Metropolitan Police in London, to make sure he settled in to his temporary home with us. Louis's end destination was to be Roland's other sanctuary in Brantome, France, where ex-British Police Horses, which have been retired from England, are cared for.

Louis was to stay with us for a while, to enable him to acclimatise to this massive change in his lifestyle. His life had involved working on the front line, on the streets of London, but now he had to get used to retirement and being in paddocks with horses he did not know. On his arrival, Louis was initially put in the small paddock next to our yard, to settle him in while he was getting his bearings. As you can see from the photo of him, he is a stunning looking horse and due to his size and personality, he was later to become one of the favourites of the many visitors to Roland's sanctuary in Brantome.

I met Louis when I arrived for my usual Wednesday and he had only been with us for one day. I was totally in awe of him, as I had never seen such a huge horse. He was much bigger than Gilly and Captain, who I thought were huge. In fact, even the girls, who have seen many horses in their time, called him a 'giant'. As for his size, well, the minimum requirement height for a Metropolitan Police horse is 16.1 hands. As a rule, they are around 17.5 hands.

What is a 'hand'[13] and how is this measured? A 'hand' is measured as four inches or 10.16 centimetres. The actual height of a horse is measured from between the horses' withers to the ground (the withers is the ridge between the shoulder blades.)

---

[13] 'Merlin' by Gordon Thorburn

So, if a horse is 18 hands, his withers are either 183 centimetres, or 6 feet from the ground. I am no expert, but I would say Lewis was at least 17.5 hands, maybe more – let's just stick to my earlier observation that he was a giant of a horse.

Unfortunately, my first experience of him was not a pleasant one and an even worse one for my young dog, who had only just started coming up to the sanctuary. He was nervous of these animals, as he had never been around horses before.

By early Wednesday morning, Louis was more than very keen to get out of the small paddock. He wanted to get into the much larger paddock next door, where Comic and Copperfield lived. Only a gate stood in the way of this enticing new life. What happened during the simple process of opening that gate and letting Louis out, nearly cost my dog his life and it was entirely my fault.

Louis was, understandably, champing at the bit to get into the larger paddock and meet some new friends. One of our girls was at the gate, ready to open it and she was anxious not to delay, as Louis had sensed he was going somewhere and was thundering around the small space impatiently.

I was standing with Micala, by the opening part of the gate and both of us were in the paddock Louis was being let into. Milo was by my side and I had told him to sit down, which he did. What I should have done, was shut him in the car, as we didn't know anything about this horse and weren't sure what he would do during this process. I could have put Milo on the lead, but I didn't think. As the gate was opened, two things happened at once and at eye watering speed. Louis shot out on full throttle, both turbos' wide open and at that very moment, Milo panicked and ran from me, right across the path of this charging horse.

In that split second, I shut my eyes not wanting to see the carnage I was sure would happen as a result of my foolishness. I think, that as Milo rushed across the horse's path, Louis reacted unbelievably quickly and jumped over him, to avoid colliding with him. However, one of Louis's massive back hooves clipped Milo's front leg, as he soared over my dog. As the horse thundered on, Milo let out a howl of sheer agony and I thought I might be sick, as I feared he may be seriously injured.

Milo responded to my frantic screams to come to me, limping back on three legs, ears flat to his head. My first thought was 'thank God he is not too badly hurt/dead', then the realisation hit me with a heavy cloud of dread, that Terrina, my other half, would kill me for exposing our beloved dog to this danger. Whilst she had been keen for me to take Milo up to the sanctuary, so he would get used to the horses and be able to be with me all day, this came with a massive caveat – be careful with him.

I looked at Milo's front leg and at his knee. I was sickened to see all the skin had been skimmed off a large area and it was quickly swelling. He allowed me to flex it, but he couldn't weight bear on it. Shouting an apology at Micala for leaving the sanctuary on my day to do the chores, I bundled him into my car. The tiny lanes leading from the sanctuary to the village of Manaton are not conducive to speeding, so this bit of the journey was very stressful. Once I was out on the slightly larger road at Manaton, I let my Audi S3 come into her own and was soon across the moors and out on the A38, where, during my journey home, I was relived not to see any Policemen.

Plymouth is nearly forty miles away from the sanctuary, but even at high speed, the journey seemed to take an age. I screeched into my vets' car park and bundled Milo out of the car, running into the waiting room. The staff ushered me in to see the vet immediately and after a lengthy examination, he concluded that Milo's leg was not broken. I nearly fainted with relief. He was given painkillers and anti-inflammatory drugs. However, this relief was short lived, as once home, I had to ring Terrina to tell her what happened. I didn't want her to be too shocked when she walked in after work, to see our boy wrapped in blankets, feeling very sorry for himself on the sofa.

Dialling her work number, I braced myself for an onslaught, but she was very understanding. I think she could tell how upset I was. Milo did have to go back to the vets a few days later, as he still wouldn't put any weight on his bad leg. He had an x-ray, but the diagnosis was the same, no break. It took him a long time to walk properly and even longer to get his confidence back around the horses. To this day, he gives all of them a very wide berth and is alert at all times.

As for Louis, the rest of the time he spent at the sanctuary was uneventful after the incident with Milo. He adapted to country life very well and a few weeks later, he was deemed to be ready to be transported to France. He went over with Copperfield and Comic.

Lewis is now very happy in France, mixing very well with the other retired Police Horses.

Louis, ex-Police horse with Cracker and Freddie – Dolly in the back ground.

Louis – Gentle Giant at Brantome.

FIE: ABANDONED BY GYPSIES AFTER THEY RUINED HER BACK LEGS GIG RACING.

Her story is typical of an ill-treated animal that comes to us. The events of her heart breaking abandonment and subsequent rescue attempts were recounted to Roland, the owner of our sanctuary, by Rosie, one of the two young sisters who found Fie abandoned by gypsies on the outskirts of Guilford, Essex. Fie was found starving and neglected. She also had terrible injuries to her legs from being hobbled by wire. This barbaric practice restricts the movement of a horses back legs when they are raced on roads by their gypsy owners. As if she hadn't suffered enough from this over the years, she had cigarette burns on her body.

Rosie told Roland, that one Sunday in October she arrived at her place of work on an Industrial estate in Guildford and found that the night before, a group of eight horses had been abandoned there.

Rosie immediately tried to ascertain how and when these horses had turned up. She began by speaking to other companies in the vicinity and she asked to see their CCTV footage of the previous day. She saw that a large vehicle had been driven onto the estate and had released a large group of horses. She immediately rang the RSPCA and Horse Watch.

Although she informed them of the horses' poor condition, she was told by the RSPCA that they would not come out to collect them unless they were on a public highway or were causing a danger to the public. So, as the horses were wandering around grazing outside the different car dealerships on the industrial estate, the RSPCA refused to come out. At the end of the day, all the horses had found their way to the fields behind the industrial estate and were grazing.

When Rosie went to work Monday, she looked into the fields where the horses had been the previous day and saw only one of the horses was left. She later found out that on the Sunday night, one horse had found its way on to the main road between Guildford and Woking and was hit by a motorcyclist. The horse was put down due to its injuries and the motorcyclist was taken to hospital. One has to wonder if this accident could have been avoided if the RSPCA had been able to respond to Rosie's urgent call for help the previous day.

Throughout Monday, Rosie kept seeing this chestnut horse in the field. She tried the RSPCA again but was told the same as the previous day - there was nothing they could do unless the horse was on a public highway.

Rosie realised no one else was interested in helping this poor horse, so she rang her sister Tabitha who was a riding teacher and owned her own horse. Later that day, Tabitha came over with hay, carrots and fresh water for the abandoned horse, which was so hungry, she came straight over to her and let her sister check her over. Now the horse was in close proximity, they could see how skinny she was and they were also horrified to see a number of cigarette burns on her and found there were other injuries on her body.

Tabitha decided she couldn't leave this poor creature out another night and immediately phoned a few friends, to try and get a horse box. Unfortunately, no one could help at such short notice and as they didn't want to take the chance of leaving her overnight again, they decided to risk walking her to Tabitha's' stables, which were three miles away. This was a very brave decision, as they did not know how the horse was going to react during the walk and by this time it was getting dark.

Tabitha put a head collar on the horse and attached a lead rope. The first problem they had to deal with was getting the nervous horse out of the field. The only way out was through parked cars on the garage forecourt and unfortunately, the frightened horse wasn't having any of it. The girls were also worried the horse might panic and damage the cars. They were not sure whether the horse was refusing to be led that way because she knew she wouldn't fit, or whether she was just scared. Eventually they found a larger gap between the cars and were able to coax the horse through.

Now the horse was safely out of the vicinity of the garage, there was a second problem the girls had to deal with. Darkness was falling very quickly, so Tabitha asked the friend who had driven her over to rescue the horse, to drive very slowly behind the two girls and the horse with her car headlights on full beam, to light the road ahead. Rosie's partner drove in front, to warn oncoming traffic to slow down. Once they reached the main road they followed a footpath next to it for about a mile, then to their relief, they were able to join some country lanes which led to the stables.

Whilst these country lanes were quieter, they were pitch black, as there were no street lamps. The girls were glad of the two cars' headlights. Walking through the dark lanes, eerily lit by the cars lights, the girls felt they were in a surreal situation, but they both agreed they had to save this horse. They couldn't have left this poor horse out another night.

To their surprise and relief, the horse continued to behave well, as if she knew the girls were saving her and were kind people. The last half mile of their journey was down a very narrow bridle path and without the two cars to guide them, the girls had to use the lights from their mobile phones.

When they finally reached the stables, the two girls were flooded with relief that they had been able to get the horse to safety without any incidents. They decided they should give the horse a name and thought it apt she should be named after one of the cars at the garage where she had been found, so she was named Fiesta.

Tabitha took Fiesta into a stable and fed her. The next day, she wormed her and arranged for her vet and a chiropractor to check her over, because Fiesta had a few problems with her back legs. The vet told the girls that her back legs were damaged as a result of the years of abuse from pulling a cart at high speed on the road. It was established that she could never be ridden but the vet gave Tabitha some physiotherapy techniques to help improve Fiesta's walking.

A few months later, Tabitha was told by the riding school, who owned the stables where Fiesta was now settling in well, that she had to find a new home for her as they couldn't provide the stable for her any longer. The girls were devastated, particularly Tabitha as she had grown very fond of Fiesta. She was desperate to keep her, however, she had her own horse to look after, so Tabitha decided to advertise Fiesta on a 'Pre-Loved' website to be a companion for someone.

During her time at the stables Fie had got on very well with the other horses, people and children, responding to the love, care and attention the people there lavished on her, so Tabitha was confident she would be able to find a good home for her. A few people responded to the advert and some days later, someone came to see her and said they would like to have her. Following sad goodbyes, Fiesta left the riding stables with a new rug, head collar and lead reign the sisters had bought her during her stay.

Rosie and Tabitha were hopeful of a happy ending for this poor horse, who had come to them so badly frightened and abused, however, it was not to be. A few days later, Tabitha received a phone call from Fiesta's new owners, asking whether she thought Fiesta was rideable. Tabitha told these people that she had clearly stated in the advert the horse could not be ridden. One week later, Fiesta was dumped again.

Tabitha only realised this had happened when she received a call from her boss, who told her some stables nearby had rung to say a chestnut mare had been dumped off with them and did they know anything about it? Tabitha immediately went to the stables and was shocked to find it was Fiesta. Whilst the owners of these stables at first appeared sympathetic, Tabitha was told in no uncertain terms that if a new home wasn't found for this horse in a week, she would be shot.

This poor horse had spent her life being abused by gypsies, was then abandoned by them and since her rescue, had been to three different places in less than a few months. Now she was facing certain death.

Tabitha broke down in tears and rang her sister Rosie. They had grown to love Fie and were determined to find her a new home. Rosie began a frantic internet search for horse sanctuaries and came across the DHAPS website. She sent an appeal to find out if they could take Fiesta. Rosie received a call the next day from Debbie, who ran the sanctuary at that time. Debbie had discussed this with her father Roland and they both agreed that Fiesta had suffered enough and deserved a permanent, safe and loving home. They would send a horse box up to London to collect Fiesta within the next few days. Rosie broke down in tears again and says she spent most of that day crying with joy and relief.

Roland was amazed to find out later that his was the only horse charity to respond to Rosie's plea. He thanked Rosie and Tabitha for their courage and determination. Many people would have looked the other way, but they had rescued her twice. Roland has since found out that the remaining animals were sold through local sales and we all hate to think what has happened to those poor unfortunate horses. Fiesta was, very, very lucky.

Roland hired a horse box to collect Fie and she arrived at the sanctuary just few weeks before me, on 22nd July, 2011. When I first set eyes on Fie, my heart went out to her, she was so very nervous and had a really sad, forlorn look in her eyes. I fell in love with her instantly and set my heart on establishing a relationship with her.

Each Wednesday, once my chores were finished, I would spend ages trying to get close to Fie, but every time I got close to her, she would walk away. Talking to her in a soft voice, I would edge forwards towards her very slowly, but the minute I extended my hand to give her a carrot, she would turn and walk off. Following several weeks of this routine and many hours of patience, she tentatively started to take a few carrots, but only if I held one piece at a time between my thumb and forefinger, my arm at full stretch so I was not too close. If I tried feeding her from my open hand, or made a sudden move she thundered off.

As the months passed, she began to follow me when I walked away from her, but if I stopped and walked back to her, she walked off. She did not trust me yet, but I hoped she was gradually warming to me. The other three girls were also trying to spend some time with her. We needed to be able to get a head collar on her and be able to lead her, in case we needed to move her or she needed to be stabled. She also would need to see the farrier, so it was important to continue with the bonding, handling and trusting process.

Initially, Fie had been placed in our biggest paddock with Shannon, Holly, Robin and Lucky. Shannon was slightly bigger than Fie, but Robin, Lucky and Holly were small Shetlands. Fie made friends with Holly immediately, but she showed no interest in the other horses. Shannon began to bully her, particularly when food was around, so Sian moved Fie into another paddock, with three other horses - Haidi, Cider, and Vera.

Unfortunately, Fie was bullied in there as well, particularly at feed times by both Vera and Haidi. I was worried that she wasn't getting her full ration of food. The weather was getting colder, so it was important we maintained the weight she had put on since joining us. At feeding times during her first winter with us, I took a full feed bowl down to her paddock and with this, encouraged her to walk away from the other horses. Once at a safe distance, I then sat on the floor holding her food bowl in my lap while she ate. My idea was that she would get to eat all of her food and this would also help strengthen my bond with Fie. Either her hunger overcame her nerves or she had come to trust me enough to eat from the bowl in my lap. Probably the former. This became a regular routine with us, whatever the weather. I also made sure she ate her share of the hay we were providing in the colder weather too.

As time passed, she gained a suiter in the form of Lewis, our ex show jumper, the horse who was filmed by Channel four. He became besotted with her. Our diary records that he was "obsessed with Fie." Judging by the amount of weeing she was doing when they met over the adjoining gate (this is something female horses apparently do when they are interested in a male horse) the feelings were mutual! The girls even referred to Fie in our diary as a "tart".

At this time, I was becoming very worried about Fie being in the same paddock as Vera. Vera was a very unpredictable horse, sometimes friendly, but on more occasions than not, she would charge at us or the other horses, usually for no particular reason. Making a fuss of Fie became impossible because Vera always noticed and immediately came thundering over, which made Fie run off and me want to follow her.

It was normal practice for all of us to keep a wheel barrow between us and Vera and if that failed, we would make a hasty retreat either over the nearest gate, or up into a hedge, to avoid being bowled out of the way or worse, kicked. Vera's behaviour resulted in all of us having less physical contact with Fie, which was not what any of us wanted.

One day I was on my way out of Fie's paddock when I glanced over at Vera, to make sure I knew where she was. Her menacing gaze was fixed just in front of me and down to the right. With a sinking feeling, I recognised her 'pre-charge' look and with increasing alarm, I followed her gaze down to where my dog Milo sat waiting for me, oblivious as to what was about to happen next.

Just as I shouted "run Milo" Vera launched herself forward and as Milo picked up speed, so did Vera. She was, to my horror, hot on his heels and he just managed to scrape himself under the post and rail fencing as she skidded to a halt just an inch away from the fence. Milo was already wary of Vera as this was not the first time he had been chased by her, so I was thankful, he had recognised my warning shout immediately.

When it became obvious Vera was not ever going to let us near Fie, I asked Sian if she could either move Fie or move Vera. In Sept 2012, Vera was moved in with the Dartmoor's, Rudolf and Snowflake. Within a few weeks, with Vera out of the picture, Sian, myslef and the other girls were able to resume their attempts at grooming Fie. We starting with her neck, slowly working our way along her poor battered, scarred body and after a few weeks, Fie was also allowing Micala to pat her. We were all so very pleased with our progress with this scared horse. I was beside myself one Wednesday when Fie allowed me to put my arms round her neck and cuddle her. I stayed there with her head resting on my shoulder for nearly half an hour.

Sian began to make a habit of taking a lead rope down to Fie's paddock when she took the food down. She ran it along Fie's back so she became used to this and was not nervous of it, so when we eventually got a head collar on her, she would trust us when we attached the rope. With winter approaching, it was critical we were able to catch Fie and get a head collar and lead reign on her, because she would need to be rugged up.

As time went by and Fie slowly became more comfortable around us, we decided it was time to attempt to get a head collar on her - but we were always unsuccessful. Although she was beginning to trust us enough to accept carrots, allow me to hold her food bowl and stroke her, she became very nervous if we departed from the norm. However, a few weeks after we started to approach Fie with a head collar and try and catch her, Micala had a major achievement. She succeeded not only in catching Fie, but she also picked her feet out as well. Result! I thought that was very brave of her to attempt this, with a horse who was very nervous and un-predicable. Leanne wrote in our diary that month that she "had a cuddle with Fie today, she is really starting to come round."

However, our hopes for further progress were dashed in September, when none of us could get near Fie to give her the additional feeds she needed, as she had dropped some weight. A horse can drop weight for a number of reasons: worms (although our horses are regularly wormed) or if they are not rugged up in winter, as their energy goes on keeping warm and they can lose weight. In addition, stress can bring on weight loss, as do some illnesses.

We thought in Fie's case, it was probably due to a mixture of stress and the fact the other horses gobbled their food down and then shoved her out of the way to eat hers. Whist I stood over her every Wednesday to ensure she got her share, Sian and Micala did not always have the time to do this and we did not want to risk trying to tie Fie up. In the end, it was decided that at feeding times, we would segregate Fie from the other horses, so she could feed in peace. All we had to do was entice her over to a gate with her food and she would willingly walk through.

A few weeks later we needed to get a head collar on her, because the farrier was coming and we wanted her hooves shaved back. The three of us managed to get her into the small top paddock with a food bribe, but although we got close enough to get a head collar on her, she was terrified at being put in a small enclosure. We were very concerned when she started cantering around snorting and showing signs of severe stress. We thought she might attempt to jump the fence, so we had no choice but to let her out. She did not get to see the farrier this time round. However, at the end of October, she allowed her feet to be picked out again and we felt this was another major milestone with her.

Later in the year, Sian decided to bring Fie back into the large paddock, next to our yard so she would have more human contact. This was to prove a key decision and one which would speed up Fie's rehabilitation process. It also proved to be a timely move, because one morning a few weeks later, Sian arrived at the Sanctuary and was concerned to find Fie cold and shivering in the pouring rain.

Sian knew she had to get Fie in to one of our stables and get her dried off and rugged up. However, Fie was still so very nervous and she had never been in our yard, let alone in one of our stables. She is also a big horse and it was going to be very difficult for Sian to get Fie through the other horses, through the gate and into the yard. Then she had the task of getting Fie into a stable. This was potentially a dangerous undertaking not just because Fie was unpredictable, but because Sian was up there on her own. An accident which resulted in Sian being injured would have serious consequences.

It took Sian an hour and a half just to entice Fie into the yard and another hour to get her into a stable. By this time, Sian was drenched and also very cold, but buoyed up in the knowledge that she had helped Fie to take a giant step forward in the trust department. Fie's reward was being in a dry stable, being able to eat her meal and hay without being bullied and having fresh bedding under her feet. She would be rugged up when she dried out later.

Poor Sian was now not only very cold and wet, but she was also several hours behind schedule with the feeds for the other horses and with the other chores. However despite this, before she tackled this work, she rang to tell me what she had achieved. I cried with relief – my beloved horse was now warm and dry. Not only that, she had trusted Sian to bring her in and I hoped that was the first time of many that she would allow herself to be led into the yard and stables.

Unfortunately, when Fie had finished her breakfast and munched her way through the hay, she quickly realised she was going to have to stay in the stable and she was not happy. Sian, however, was determined Fie should get used to being handled and stabled as part of her daily routine, as this would be critical for her rehabilitation and also if she became ill and had to be stabled.

Sian kept her in for about four days, during which time, she was able to groom Fie and eventually, was able to put a head collar on her and a nice warm rug. I was over the moon. To this day, I cannot thank Sian enough for her perseverance – Fie may not be the horse she is today without that. During this time, I looked forward to my Wednesdays even more, as I was also able to groom her. I was not brave enough to do this in the stable, as Fie normally started whizzing around restlessly and I was worried she may accidentally squash me against the walls of the stable. I used to lead her out into the yard, where she was happy to munch on some hay while I groomed her. I hoped that by doing this and visiting her on additional days, it would strengthen not only our bond, but confidence and trust on both sides.

We were all worried that when we had to put her out in her normal paddock with her mates, she would revert to being uncatchable again. Fortunately, Sian's insistence that Fie was caught every day and brought in for her feeds, meant that slowly Fie became consistently more approachable. During that winter Fie was brought in every day to be fed in the stable and although she was not best pleased with being confined again, her hunger was a huge motivator. She was very keen to get her head in her bowl and to be able to eat uninterrupted. Following a few days of this routine, she was found waiting at the gate to the yard to be let in.

I will never forget the first time I caught Fie and led her out of her paddock, into the yard, then into the stable to feed. It was something I thought I would never be able to do and I was so overcome, I cried. The horse must have thought I was mad. I was also beaming from ear to ear, so proud of how far my girl had come and very honoured that she now trusted me to catch her and lead her in.

Me and my girl Fie.

The farrier was, of course, another matter. Even though Fie had come a long way with us, she still hated being shut in the small paddock prior to the farrier's arrival and no matter how often we put her in there to get her used to it, she continued to go berserk and gallop around the small space on her gammy back legs, snorting and bellowing. The result was always the same - worried that she might try and jump out, crash through the gate or skid over and break one of her legs, we had to let her re-join her friends in the larger paddock.

So it was that Fie was not to have her feet done for a good few months. Eventually she allowed me to lead her up towards the yard where the farrier was, but bolted when I tried to get her into the yard. I managed to catch her again and in the end the farrier came into the paddock and managed to trim her feet whilst I was holding her. I was enormously moved that she trusted me to hold her as the farrier worked on her feet, as I could see she was very frightened. Another milestone!

Slowly, we were able to do more with her and she was an excellent patient when she got mud fever in one of her back hooves, which we had to treat. (Mud fever was explained in Cider's chapter). I was never comfortable with picking out horses' hooves at the best of times and the first time I did Fie's I was very nervous. I also had to wash her hoof out and put a poultice on it but she was very good. The bandages I put on came off within a few minutes, so I had to phone Sian and ask her to come up later and re apply it. I suppose I am to horses what Frank Spencer is to DIY.

We found over the course of the next year that Fie and horse rugs did not appear to get on. Although she stood very quietly when she was rugged, within a day, she had managed to get the straps off so we had to catch her and do them up. I always worried that if we couldn't catch her, she would get her legs caught and fall over.

On one occasion, she did just that. Of course, it had to be a Wednesday, on my shift. I arrived at the Sanctuary to find Fie lying down and approached her with my heart in my mouth. When I got closer, she did not attempt to get up, which made me feel sick with apprehension and set alarm bells ringing in my head. I soon spotted the trouble. She had got her back leg tangled in one of the leg straps of her rug

I approached her talking calmly and quietly and sat down by her side, telling her I was going to untangle the strap, so she should lie still. Thankfully, she did and she was able to stand up as soon as I freed her leg. I quickly straightened her rug before she trotted off to join her mates. I say "mates", but they were not at all concerned about her, munching on grass over the other side of the paddock.

Each year, the dilemma continues as to when we should rug Fie up. The risk of her getting cold without a rug always outweighs the risk of her coming a cropper getting tangled up, but all of us worry about finding her in a state, tangled up in her rug, when we arrive each day. Later I solved that worry by taking the back leg straps off.

Later in 2012, after Fie had been with us for about a year, Micala made my day by asking if I could "work with Fie, as she gets on well with you." However, for a few weeks after that, Fie decided that no one would be allowed near her, so I felt a bit deflated. Her behaviour was very inconsistent.

The next drama unfolded when I arrived at the sanctuary one Wednesday morning, to find Fie had gotten into the next paddock, as one of the residents there had kicked a cross pole down. Fie decided the other paddock looked more inviting than her own – even though Vera ruled that area. Having a fence between her and Vera had given Fie a false sense of security, that perhaps Vera could be her mate after all. So Fie must have stepped over the bottom pole and went to join her old enemy. Bad mistake.

As I walked down to her paddock with her breakfast, I was puzzled to see that Fie was in Vera's paddock and my heart sank. As I drew closer, to my horror, I saw Fie take off at speed, with Vera in hot pursuit. Fie's back legs are very un-steady at the best of times, but with Vera chasing her round the paddock relentlessly, I was distraught she may slide over and break one of her legs as she tore around the muddy, un-even paddock which was also littered with boulders. I held my breath and watched.

Each time Fie stopped, sweating and snorting, Vera charged after her again. Angie, a friend who comes up with me each

Wednesday and I hatched a plan. She would go back up to the barn and get a hay net to distract Vera, while I put some rope across the gap in the fence as a temporary repair and keep an eye on Fie. Then, when she returned, Angie would feed Vera the hay and Vera would be so busy eating, she would not notice me enticing Fie back out of the gate, to the safety of her paddock. It seemed like a great plan. If only.

Apart from Vera, my other problem was the heavy wooden gate which separated Fie's and Vera's paddock. It was not hinged, but kept in place by ropes. There was also no latch – it was tied up with old rope in two places. This would make it very difficult for me to get the gate open quickly and to keep it from falling over as I dragged it backwards, if I could get Fie to come over. Also, it would be difficult to shut quickly, should Vera be charging up behind Fie. As if that were not bad enough, the gate opened inwards, which meant there was a real danger I would be sandwiched between the gate and Fie if she tore past before I got the gate open wide enough.

I remember there was a lot of swearing (from me) and arm waving, because Vera was not to be fooled by the bribe of the hay net. Carrots didn't work either. Angie had walked quite a long way away from the gate I wanted to get Fie out of, but each time I called Fie and tried to open the gate, Vera came racing over and chased Fie away. I tried to get between Vera and Fie, but as soon as I got close to Fie, she saw Vera galloping over and ran off.

I have no idea what finally made Fie respond to my frantic calls as I opened the gate for the hundredth time. She came thundering over so fast, I only just got the gate open wide enough for her to dash through. I shut my eyes and prayed there was enough space for the both of us.

Getting her back into her own paddock had taken over an hour and during this process there had been a certain amount of trust on both sides. Fie trusted me to open the gate in time as she accelerated through and I put my safety in her hands, hoping she didn't squash me against the gate in her desperation to get back in her own paddock.

I apologised to Angie for my foul language (which would have put a builder to shame) and we spent the next hour putting the cross poles back up, securing them with nails and running electric tape along the horses' side of the fence, to discourage Vera from kicking the poles down again.

Early in February 2014 Fie became lame, with pus coming out of her toe. Sian immediately stabled her, so thank goodness she had worked hard to get her used to being confined prior to this. Sian's diary entry for that day stated: "Fie is not very happy being stabled and has already started destroying it." Bute, a painkilling powder, was added to her food, but as usual, she refused to eat it. Even the addition of apple sauce did not disguise what was clearly a horrible taste.

In August, 2014, our diary shows: "Fie in a strange mood, won't come in to feed." The next day, she started limping on her back, left leg and the vet was called out for her. His diagnosis was an 'inflamed fetlock' (swollen ankle to you and me) and so it was, Fie found herself back in the stable again, for two weeks this time and back on Bute twice daily.

This did nothing to improve her mood at first, but after a few days, she calmed down and settled into the new routine. Having a hay net and a bowl of food to herself helped and she got lots of attention from Sian, me, Julie and Bryan. Julie and Bryan had joined us as volunteers shortly after Ciders accident, as Micala and Leanne had left by this time and we needed extra pairs of hands.

I found Fie a nightmare to muck out, because although she was now calmer in the stable, she became restless when being mucked out and I worried about getting squashed when she did a round of the inside of the stable with me still in it. Sian suggested leading her out into the yard and tying her up whilst I mucked her out. Why didn't I think of that? If brains were dynamite, I would not have enough to blow my hat off.

By October of that year, Fie was again back in her stable, following a fall. I was at the sanctuary when it happened. When she had finished her breakfast, Fie raced down the slope to the bottom of her paddock to get through the open gate to join her mates, who were in the far paddock.

Unfortunately she was going at such a pace, she skidded on the mud. Her back went down and she fell badly, sliding through the gate on her side. I felt sick with dread, because although she got up reasonably quickly, she was limping when she walked off. I rang Sian and asked her to look at Fie closely when she arrived in the morning. As Fie was still limping in the morning, Sian called out Kevin, our vet, who diagnosed a pulled tendon, so Fie was once again stabled and on Bute.

By the end of November, Fie was out again, but was still being brought in each day to feed, so her leg could be rested. Whilst she was not too happy about this arrangement, it was furthering her trust in us, enabling her to have a lot more human contact and of course this meant she could eat in peace.

Towards the end of 2015, I let my concentration lapse whilst leading Fie, which resulted in a trip to casualty with a suspected broken wrist. It made me realise how complacent I had become around our horses. Fie had been on Bute again, due to the arthritis flaring up again in her knees. In order to ensure she ate her food with the Bute in it and was not pushed aside by the other horses, each day she was led to a space between two of the gates in her paddock and fed there.

I had fed the other three horses in the paddock and I was leading Fie over to the two gates when the accident happened. Stupidly, I led Fie between Shannon (who was eating) and the fence. I am not exactly sure what caused Fie to suddenly barge me out of the way and take off at speed, as my other mistake had been to allow Fie to walk behind me. I think Shannon must have lunged at Fie and Fie took off in a panic.

It was like being hit by a brick wall and I fell awkwardly on my left wrist. I cried out in agony. The pain was so bad, I thought I was going to be sick. With my wrist quickly swelling, my only concern was that I needed to catch Fie and get her in to feed. I caught her, apologising for my stupid mistake and managed to get her in-between the two gates to feed. Not sure how I managed it, but I also took the opportunity to put a new head collar on her.

Finishing the chores was a bit of a challenge for me, but we got it all done. Angie then insisted we went straight back to Plymouth to get my wrist x-rayed. Staff at the Cumberland Centre examined the x-rays' and thought it might be broken, so a temporary plaster was put on and an appointment was made for me to attend Derriford Hospital a few days later for more x-rays.

Angie had to drive my jeep home, because apparently, your insurance is null and void if you drive with any sort of support on your wrist.

This incident was a wake-up call, not only for me, but for Sian and Julie. We realised we did take risks up there and needed to be more careful – Sian admitted she didn't always carry her mobile phone with her, often leaving it in the barn; but she has it in her pocket at all times now.

The most worrying thing about the whole incident was my having to tell Terrina, my other half. I know she worries about my going up there, because it is risky, especially when I am on my own. I sort of under exaggerated my injuries and said I had slipped over in the mud.

Luckily, further x-rays showed my wrist was not broken, but it was still hurting some five months later. Suffice to say, I do not take any risks up there now and if I am honest, the whole thing dented my confidence quite a bit. When leading any horse, they are now slightly in front of me, so I can see what is going on.

"How much longer do I have to stay in here, mum?"

Around 2015, I asked Roland if I could adopt Fie. I wanted to keep her at the sanctuary as there wasn't anywhere in Plymouth close to where I lived where I could keep her and I didn't think I had enough confidence, experience and knowledge to look after her.

Also, we knew how neurotic she was and we didn't know how she would take the journey or react to a strange place. We agreed she would be happier staying with her mates at the Sanctuary. Roland refused my offer of paying for Fie's food, because of "all the hard work you do for us" but he agreed I could help out with vets bills, any supplements or medication she might need and I would pay for her farrier and worming costs. I knew Fie could never be re-homed, but at least I now had some say over her care and which paddock she was put in.

Due to Fie's ailments and the fact she has never, ever, given me any sort of verbal greeting when I approach her, I wanted to know if she was happy at the sanctuary. So, in March 2016, I asked Karen, the lady who runs 'Touch 2, Talk 2, Heal' if she could come up and communicate with Fie. Karen is what many might call a 'Horse Whisperer', who started healing horses and about six months into this, she discovered she could communicate with them. She has since expanded her work to all domestic animals.

I was excited at the opportunity to be able to communicate with my horse. I wanted to know a bit more about her back ground, if she was happy and if she was in any pain anywhere, so we could address that. I also wanted to find out why she didn't like being stabled.

Was there any food we were not giving her, which she would like to have? I wanted her to know she was safe at the sanctuary and that it would be her permanent home, now I had adopted her. In addition to this, I had been reading some of the cases Karen had written about on her Facebook page and had learnt that sometimes if a horse was unhappy and was able to communicate why, it helped in their recovery. Fie always looks so sad, no matter how much attention she gets and it was tearing me up.

I wanted to know if there was anything we did, which she didn't like. So many questions. I got Terrina to come up on the day of Karen's arrival, so she could read the questions out and write down the answers, as I would be busy hanging on to Fie. Before you read about what happened in this session, it is important to point out that Karen knew absolutely nothing about Fie prior to her arrival.

A few minutes before Karen arrived, I brought Fie into the yard and into a stable. As soon as Karen saw Fie, her first words were: "Oh my goodness, she is high maintenance." She opened the stable door and began to communicate with Fie and within a few minutes said: "Ok, you can come out, we will do our work in the yard."

As she led Fie out of the stable, Karen said: "Yes, you are staying here." Fie had asked whether this was to be her home now. However, Fie told Karen that she would be happy if she left the sanctuary, as long as she had a friend with her. Apparently, she likes Rudolph and Robin – she says Rudolph is a bit thick but chills her out and she understands that Robin is blind.

Fie 'told' Karen she was born on April 23rd and is 23 going on 24. This bit of information suspended my belief for a while about what I was being told, as I don't understand how a horse could possibly know the date she was born and how old she was. Fie went on to tell Karen that she had had two foals, one of which was a male. He was a seven year old gelding when she was abandoned. The father was a coloured cob called Stanley.

Fie asked Karen if it would be ok to have her hay net whilst the session was taking place, so the one from the stable was brought over and tied to the gate.

Fie then began to tell Karen about her past. She had been trotted really fast on roads as she was very sure footed. I knew this piece of information to be true, as we knew her past history of being owned by gypsies and we knew her back legs were in bad shape. Fie said she had been tethered by the side of the road and hated that. She had been hit by a man with a driving stick whilst she was gig racing. She told Karen she is used to being handled by men and her owner had two daughters, one of which was called Sarah. Fie had also been hit when she was stabled, which she said is why she doesn't like being stabled now.

She told Karen that one day, she fell during a high action trot – which means her back legs were faster than the front ones - and went down on her right knee. Karen felt this knee and was able to identify scar tissue there then on to her right side. She was 17 at the time and had been with her owner since she was three. There must be some truth in this information, because Fie always gets arthritis in her right knee.

She told Karen she was a very proud horse, as she had been 'high ranking', the leader of a herd of about five to seven horses. I have to say I was very surprised at this piece of information, because at the time of Karen's visit and still to this day, she is not pack leader here at the sanctuary.

I was shocked and saddened to hear that Fie misses and still has much fondness for her previous owner – someone who did not treat her at all kindly. She said it was because of the relationship they had. Although he was affectionate with her in private, in public he was indifferent. She does not bear him a grudge for what he did for her. She believes that when he made the initial decision to keep her, even though she had damaged a tendon racing, he was keeping her alive. However, this callous man later changed his mind and abandoned her due to this injury. Apparently, he was too fond of her to have her shot, so he decided the better alternative was to abandon her with those other horses on that industrial estate, hoping she was rescued and given a good home. Not fond enough of her to find a decent home though.

Fie admitted she had a bad time, but told Karen she wasn't abused the way some of the other horses were. I shudder to think what those other horses went through then, as Fie had cigarettes stubbed out on her and was pretty much raced until she dropped. She was 'cross hobbled' while gig racing, which is a method of strapping the legs so the horse cannot canter.

Her physical condition and scars bear witness to the terrible way she was treated, so I am confused and upset that she appeared to be happy with the man who owned and raced her – in fact she still holds this man in great affection.

As well as the damage to her side and right knee, Karen identified a lot of worm damage and Fie told her it was Red worm. Karen laughed at the fact Fie knew what colour her worms were!

Karen also identified a 'locking stifle'. A stifle is the horse equivalent of our knee, but it is hidden at the top of their legs. Horses can lock their own stifles so they can rest or sleep standing up. However, sometimes when these are 'locked', they won't release, so the horse stumbles when trying to walk forward after a prolonged period of standing. This stifle can be released by walking the horse backwards. Karen also said Fie had a 'tightness in her head', which was due to stress.

Karen felt the colour blue while running her hands over Fie's stomach area. She concluded that Fie suffers from stomach pain and acid in her stomach due to ulcer damage, which is why she never feels full.

Fie asked if we were going to 'get anything for my arthritis?' Karen recommended Cartrophen Injections. As you read in earlier paragraphs, normally one or both of her knees swell up on the approach of winter. The vet has been called about this, but apparently, injections are a short term fix. At the time of writing, we now put her on Danilon when her arthritis flares up, which is an anti-inflammatory/pain killer powder, a nicer tasting alternative to the bitter taste of Bute. She will eat all her food with this in, which keeps her pain levels down.

Karen told me I need to keep the lead rope looser when I lead her and I need to be calmer round her and take more control. She thinks Fie is very bossy, so I need to be strong so she is confident with me. This is right, there are occasions even now, after over eight years at the sanctuary, that I do lack confidence.

Fie told Karen she is used to fighting for food, but would prefer to be put in with the smaller horses, as they are not so stroppy, then she would not be bullied. Karen asked me what, if any supplements we were giving Fie and I said Cod Liver Oil, seaweed and garlic powder. Karen said we should never give any horse Cod Liver Oil because the liver does not digest it. Vegetable or Sunflower oil is fine though. As a result of Karen's advice, Fie has herbs and a gastric aid powder to help with her digestion in her feed.

Fie told Karen she is "coping with the weather now", but doesn't "like the driving rain." She told Karen that she doesn't get bothered with midges here, because the land is higher and it is breezier at the sanctuary. She said she wanted a nice thick rug, with a fleece collar and we were to make sure the back strap was tight, as she doesn't like the wind going up under the rug over her back. I went out straight away and bought her a new rug.

I came in for some criticism. Apparently, I start things and don't finish them. Her comments are justified, as I had been promising to buy her a new rug but had forgotten. I asked if Fie understood I had adopted her and Karen said she "kind of" understands that but asked if I now 'owned her'; why do I only come up once a week? I thought that was a bit unfair of her, as I go up twice a week in the summer to see and groom her and even in the winter, I try and get up twice a week. Perhaps she hasn't the concept of the fact I do a seventy-six mile round trip, each time I go up there.

Also, she said sometimes I don't go back to her and say goodbye before I leave the sanctuary. "You go too quietly" and I should tell her when I am coming up next. Karen was spot on with that point. Sometimes, if I am really tired when I finish, I don't make the trek over to say goodbye to her if she is in one of the far paddocks.

I now make a point of going into her paddock and giving her treats and a cuddle before I leave. I also tell her when I am coming up next. Apparently, Fie is not fussed on the new purple head collar I bought her. She prefers the red one as it fits better. Excuse me.

I also mutter a lot, so she can't hear what I am saying sometimes. I was surprised to hear that after all that negative stuff, Fie also said she is worried she is not enough for me. I love the bones of that horse – she has no worries there.

I have always called Fie 'My Girl'; which apparently (and spookily) is what her gypsy owner used to call her. He also called her his "Princess". Fie doesn't mind my singing "My Girl" to her, as long as I don't hit the high notes, as apparently she can't hear those.

She didn't mind being called Fie, as she thought that was short for Fiona, but was horrified to find out she was named after a car. When Karen had left, I moved Fie into a paddock with our smaller horses. However, she immediately became very stressed, calling for her mates, so I moved her back in with them.

What did I expect from the session with Karen and Fie? I did hope for a little indication that Fie was a bit fond of me, but got mainly criticism. I found this a bit disappointing and demoralising, but to be fair most of what she 'said' was true. On the whole, I think she is happy with us but I am trying to encourage her to stand up for herself with her fellow horses – if she was 'leader of the herd' when with the gypsies, surely she can assert herself here.

At the time of writing, I do not hear her tummy rumbling as much as it used to, so I think the herbs and supplements are working. I continue to go up and see her an extra day when I can. In the winter, the weather is not very conducive to standing around chatting to her, so I don't go up on many additional days, unless I am asked to help when the farrier comes. I reassure her that she is more than enough for me and I hope I am for her. She must get bored with all this talk, because once she has finished her food, she is off to tackle one of the hay nets we put in the shelter for her and her herd.

Her new rug with the neck piece lasted very well, but she sometimes got the back leg straps tangled round her back legs. Following a spell when I had to rub cream into her back legs where the strap had rubbed them, I decided that when the rug came off in the warmer weather, I would cut the leg straps off. I did and am delighted that since then, we have had no problems with her rug.

In October, 2016, Fie's arthritis flared up again – as it does this time every year, when the cold, damp weather starts – and she went slightly lame. We immediately started her off again with Danilon; but we have to do this in a controlled manner. There is a fine line between relieving the swelling and pain and preventing the horses' dependency on this drug, which, if given in too high quantities, too regularly, can also cause liver damage. So initially, Danilon was given once daily for a week, then only a few times a week, then down to once a week. Then none at all.

Towards the end of 2016, Sian arrived to find Fie had fallen and got herself wedged under the post and rail fencing in her paddock. She rang me, but I was out on the moors with Milo and it would be some time before I could get home and back out to Southcott. She rang Julie, who on arrival, went over to ask farmer Brian if he could help. Thankfully, he could and thanks to the efforts of the three of them - Fie was soon free and tucking into her breakfast.

By early December, Fie's Danilon intake had been gradually reduced, and by the week before Christmas, she was not limping and the swelling on her knee was greatly reduced. At the end of December, Sian records in our diary that 'Fie very sweet today.' Probably due to the fact that at last, she was not in any pain.

However, in January 2017, Fie is back on Danilon again for her swollen and painful right knee. In May as her back legs were very stiff, it was back on the Danilon again. During this time, all of us were leading her in for her daily feeds and she was being groomed and was used to having her feet picked out regularly. She was now very easy to catch and much less stressed about being walked across a few paddocks for her feeds.

In June, Lara suggested I buy Fie a summer rug, to keep her dry in the rain. Fie continues to be led into the yard and into a stable for her feeds. However, for some reason in September, Fie becomes very stressed and it is a battle to get her into the yard, let alone a stable. Who knows what goes on in her head to make her so changeable, so suddenly? Next, she decides not to eat all her food, so she had us all worried and wondering what the cause of this latest fad is. Danilon, the pain killer was given for a few days, in case she was in pain with her swollen knee.

Fie was to face another event, which would really freak her out. I wondered if her not eating might have something to do with her teeth. I asked Roland if the Keith, the dentist, who was called out to see Bella in February 2018, could look at Fie's teeth while he was there. He agreed that would be a good idea.

Micala was up the sanctuary early to catch Fie and Bella, get them stabled and help the dentist. She also took the pictures of Bella and Fie having their teeth done.

Keith was quick, professional and kept Fie very calm. He said that considering her age, her mouth and teeth were in very good condition. She had no wobbly teeth, just a few which needed rasping down, to prevent them getting sharper with the possibility of them cutting her cheeks and tongue.

He made an interesting discovery. Apparently, Fie is one of a third of mares who have a 'stallion fighting tooth'. These develop in the womb in some mares, due to the mix of hormones. It can sometimes indicate a head strong mare which she may have been as a youngster, and to some extent, she still is now. Stallions have them, which they use during their fights for mares during the breeding season.

Fie appeared none the worse for her experience, except she took her stress out on Bella. She gave her a hefty kick when she joined her in the paddock. This dentist had a marvellous way with both horses and even gave us discount as we are a charity. He advised another check-up for Fie in a years' time.

We hoped Fie would be back to eating all her feed after the dentist's visit, but she went into her normal post-stress mode and didn't eat for several days. At least we knew the reason wasn't teeth related.

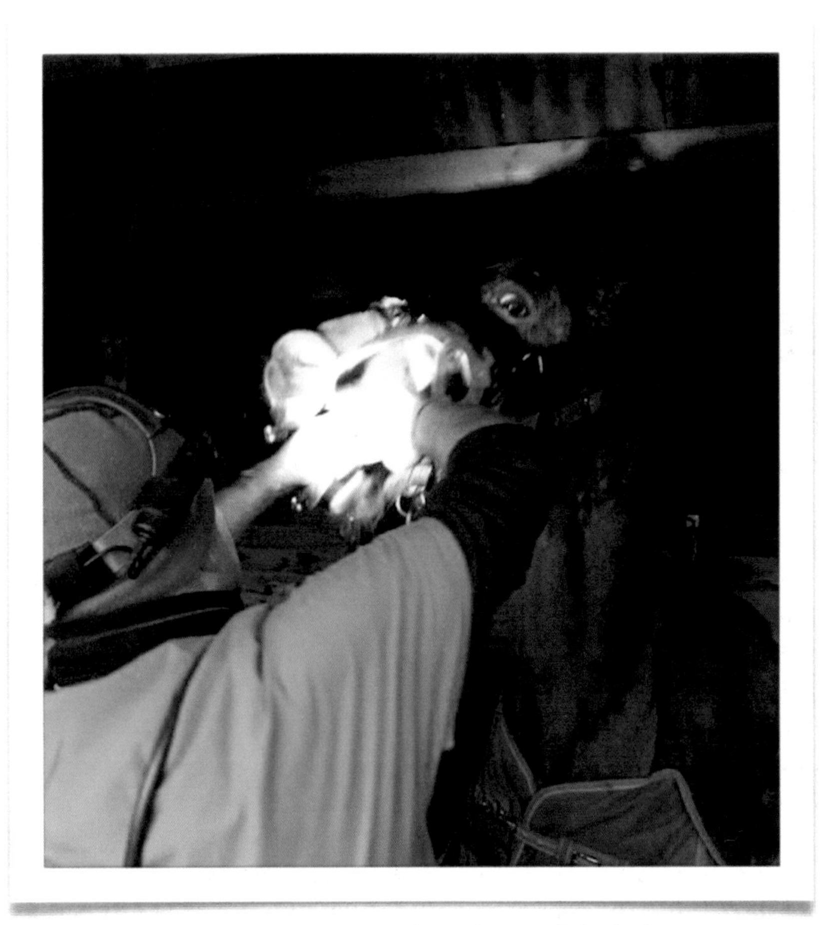

Fie not too happy to have her teeth looked at.

Any changes at the sanctuary resulted in the horses being unsettled and upset, but Fie was the horse who always reacted the worst. When her mates Shannon and Bramble were stabled mid-December, then taken from the sanctuary to be shipped over to Roland's sanctuary in France, Fie's response was to embark on another one of her not eating phases and bolting off when one of us tried to catch her.

During this time, we struggled to try and settle her, but it was a few weeks before she became approachable and started to eat properly again. Perhaps it is an example of the fragile state of her mind, caused by such ill treatment in her past. Any changes are very, very scary for her.

Shortly after Fie said goodbye to her mates Shannon and Buster, Sian left us. Fie once again became very unsettled and the predictable result was spasmodic eating. It seemed any sort of change would throw this nervous horse out. Roland and Alison volunteered to do the feeding and checking of the horses at Christmas and even this small change sent Fie off into another phase of becoming un-approachable and not eating.

Micala spends a lot of time picking the horses feet out (including Fie's) and grooming when the weather allows and this has been very good for Fie. Just after Christmas, following some debate on how we might settle Fie down, the decision was taken to move Haidi in with her. Even though Haidi wears the pants in that relationship and can bully Fie at meal times and keep her away from the hay in the shelter; Fie seems, at the time of writing to be more settled.

A few weeks later Micala arrived at the sanctuary to find Fie on the floor. On closer inspection, she found that somehow, Fie had managed to get one of her back legs stuck through and trapped in her summer rug girth strap. How on earth she managed this we do not know, but eventually Micala managed to get her free.

Fie was limping badly on the leg which had been trapped, but Micala hoped it was a simple case of loss of circulation, as the leg was quite swollen. Fie was still favouring the leg when I arrived the next day, so she was back on Danilon to reduce the pain and swelling. I crossed my fingers that this sorted my beloved horse out.

Luckily, Fie made a full recovery and apart from a small crack appearing in her right front hoof in May 2018, she has, touch wood, been free of illness and accidents. She and Haidi have been moved to one of our flat paddocks and Fie is in the best condition and frame of mind I have ever seen her. She and Haidi have a new companion, called Tessie, who came to us in the summer of last year There followed a power struggle between the new girl and Haidi, which Tess won.

As Tessie is very pushy at feed times, Micala introduced a new routine for them early in 2019. All three are tied up prior to being fed. This ensures that Tess doesn't steal the other two's feeds and also allows us to pick out feet, groom and rug up, without any resistance from either of them. In addition, it means that when the farrier arrives, they are already tied up, so we don't have to catch them. Somehow, they always know when he arrives and they can be difficult. Our farrier even walks down to their paddock, to save the stress all round of getting them up to him in the yard.

Fie has settled into her new daily routine with ease. She is affectionate and easy to handle. I think she is very happy. Long may that last.

DOLLY: WORKED AT A RIDING SCHOOL FOR DISABLED CHILDREN IN LONDON

Dolly was a dapple grey cob around 14.3 hands. We don't know her exact age but when she came to us in 2011 and the vet and dentist checked her over, they said they believed her to be around the forty year old mark. Due to lack of documentation, it is difficult to find out where Dolly originated from but we think she was owned by a family in Wales as a riding pony for their children.

Same old familiar story next. When the children had outgrown her, she was not wanted and her owners donated her to the RDA, Riding for the Disabled, in Vauxhall City Farm, London. She was again used as a riding pony there and she obtained a long service award, which Roland and Alison still have to this day, proudly displayed above her stable door.

Whilst at the City Farm she was ridden by numerous children and small adults who had learning difficulties and physical problems and we were told she was loved very much and changed many lives Although a little temperamental and always wanting her own way, she was a great favourite with the children who grew up with her.

In 2005 her career was jeopardised by a nasty group of children who were not connected with the city farm. They enticed her across her field to the fence and then threw a firework at her. She was severely burnt and traumatised, which resulted in her being sent to a livery yard to recover for a year, following intensive veterinary care. Following this awful incident, she suffered from skin problems but the people in the livery yard looked after her very well and she was able to return to the City Farm in 2006 where she continued her good work.

Shortly after the City Farm retired her in 2011, she arrived at our sanctuary. Within a very short time, Dolly had visitors who fell in love with her and wanted to take her out on loan. She left our sanctuary in April of that year, but sadly, for reasons which were not recorded, she was returned to us within a year, in June,

2012. Not a lot was recorded in our diary about Dolly, except in October 2012 the vet was called out for her, because she was itching and stamping a lot. He gave her an injection to stop her itching her legs and to kill any lice she may have had. The vet's treatment must have worked because a week later she seemed more like her old self.

Apart from that, she remained in good health and I learnt that her droopy, red, eyes was not a specific condition, but one that is seen in old horses.

I particularly liked Dolly because she was a quiet, gentle and affectionate horse, who was easy to catch and handle. I never felt intimidated by her, even when food was around, as she was never pushy or stroppy like some of the other horses could be. She lived a quiet and happy life in a large paddock with Fie, Shannon and Bramble and there were never any scraps or ill feelings between any of them.

I think it was because Dolly looked so solemn all the time that I grew so fond of her. I was pleased for Dolly, but gutted when Roland rang me in October 2012, to say they felt Dolly would benefit from the better climate at their sanctuary in France.

Roland and Alison felt that at her grand old age, this would help her old bones. Preparations began immediately to get Dolly 'transport ready' for her journey to France. Getting a horse 'transport ready' entails ensuring the details in their passports are up to date and match the chip details. She also needed 'export notes', which record who her owners are. Prior to her transportation, Dolly's medical records were checked to ensure she was up to date on her Tetanus jabs and worming. Finally, she had to be valued for insurance purposes.

We wanted to send her over to France looking dapper, so the girls bought her a new head collar and lead reign and found a decent rug for her. The day before she was due to travel, our vet was on site to check Dolly over to ensure she was physically fit for the journey. She was declared 'ready to go' on all counts. Roland and I co-ordinated the arrival of the Equine Transport lorry which was to take her to France. These are massive, air conditioned Transporters and the company who runs them very kindly gives Roland fifty percent discount on the price as he uses them very regularly and we are a charity. He still pays £500 per horse though, so it is not cheap to move our horses over to France.

I was asked if, on the day, I could take Dolly from her paddock and walk her down two miles of narrow lanes, to where the transporter would be waiting, by the green at Manaton. Due to the schedule of the transport lorry, I had to get Dolly down to the village green by 06:30 which meant all my work would have to be done in the dark.

So, while preparations were being made for Dolly's transportation, I had a bit of planning to do of my own. I did not want to have to catch Dolly and lead her across several paddocks and the two miles to the transporter on my own. So I persuaded my friend and fellow volunteer, Karen, to help me. She agreed to be ready to leave Plymouth at four thirty in the morning on the day Dolly was to be moved. I promised Karen a massive cooked breakfast at one of Plymouths best restaurants when we got back.

If only it was a simple job of catching Dolly and leading her out of the sanctuary, to the transporter. Unfortunately, there were two paddocks between hers and the entrance to the sanctuary and these were segregated by two lots of electric tape. Luckily, there were no horses in these paddocks, so the fences were not live, so our plan was to remove sections of this electric tape on our way over to get Dolly; which would mean an unobstructed journey back up through all the paddocks. I would lead Dolly across the paddocks and Karen would then reinstate the electric tape as we came through. We had to do all this in the pitch black, with only torches to guide us. We have no electricity at the sanctuary and the solar light which had been installed weeks previously only worked during the day!

Once we got Dolly in the yard, I would put her rug on and walk her through the entrance gate, which Karen would padlock after me. I would then lead Dolly, with Karen walking in front, out of the sanctuary and down the dark country lanes to Manaton, where the transporter was waiting. Not so much a big job during day light, but in the dark, very difficult. I did not know how Dolly would react to us not only turning up in probably what was to her the middle of the night, but catching her as well. Being led out of the sanctuary would also be strange for her, particularly in the dark. The only positive thing I could see from doing all this at silly o'clock in the morning, was there shouldn't be any traffic around to spook her.

The transporter was due at Manaton at 6 am, so timing was crucial. We didn't want to get to the village too early, before the transporter arrived, in case Dolly grew restless and played up. The equine transport crew, however, do not like to be kept waiting, as they have a long journey ahead of them to the ferry port, so we didn't want to be late either. Thankfully, the walk down to Manaton went without incident, although Dolly was very keen to stop regularly to snatch a quick bite from the hedge rows. As we approached the village green, relief flooded through me when I saw the lights of the waiting transporter. They were there and ready to load Dolly and begin her long journey to France.

Dolly went into the massive transporter as if she did it every day. She and the rest of the horses in the transporter would be rested, fed and watered that night in stables near the port, then they would be taken on the ferry the next day to France and Dolly would be driven down to Brantome. I was relieved that everything had gone to plan, but I was very worried about her surviving the long journey, as she was no spring chicken. I was also very sad to see her go, as I knew I would only see her again when I was on holiday in France and visited Roland's' sanctuary. As I waved the transporter off, my tears flowed as the sky began to lighten.

Karen and I returned to Plymouth for mugs of hot tea and a slap up full English breakfast, which I paid for as a thank you. She deserved that for turning out of her bed at four o'clock in the morning to help me. She definitely went above and beyond in the friendship stakes for me on that occasion.

Following our night excursion, I was moved enough to write a poem about how I led Dolly to the transporter. I was amazed, but pleased by the fact that, at 6 am on a misty, cold, very dark morning, she was not at all phased about us turning up and leading her down narrow, dark lanes. I was very moved by her trust in me.

DOLLY.

The grand old lady allowed herself to be caught.
She was being taken from her friends
        suddenly and un-expectedly,
But allowed me to lead her from them, through damp fields,
        heavy with dew.
Gently and carefully, she walked by my side,
        as darkness was pushed back slowly,
By a struggling, cloudy dawn.

With a final whinny, a farewell perhaps
        to the sanctuary, and old friends,
She allowed herself to be taken out into the small lane,
Trusting me as I led her down the un-familiar road.
Willingly and without looking back,
        she walked towards her new life.

The transporter was a welcome sight to us - but all too soon,
Dolly was standing at the bottom of the ramp.
With one final, long cuddle
        and to my words of reassurance and goodbyes,
She walked up the ramp and disappeared into the warm interior,
        smelling the fresh hay.

My tears flowed as the transporter pulled away.
I love you. Safe journey my old friend.
May you never be cold again,
        and I hope you enjoy the better climate.
May you enjoy more human company
        and the lush fields of the Dordogne.
You have worked all your life
        and you deserve to be treated like a lady.

Ann
26/10/12

Dolly, at Brantome, France.
This was taken when we were on holiday in June 2016.

I have visited the Sanctuary Roland and Alison run in France, called 'Brantome Police Horses and Friends' several times, always excited to see Dolly, Copperfield and Comic again.

During her time at Brantome Dolly had some health scares, when Roland felt he was going to lose her. She went through a phase of laying down in her paddock and not wanting to get up. However, one of their volunteers, a lady called Flo, laid down alongside Dolly in her paddock and fed her custard creams! This seemed to do the trick as Dolly was soon on her feet – no doubt with the intention of looking for some more of those biscuits. We all hoped that with the warmer weather and the one to one care she received at Brantome, this would contribute to her longevity.

Roland even joked that "Even at the grand old age of 40 she still likes the boys and still has a turn of foot. She can be a cantankerous old baggage but at her age, she has every right." So it was that Dolly lived on for another four years in France's better climate, basking in the blissful attention from Roland, his helpers and of course her friend Flo, who continued to visit Dolly regularly and kept her in custard creams.

Sadly, in October 2016, whilst carrying out his early morning checks on the stabled horses, Roland found her laying down in her stable. He immediately shouted for help, but despite the efforts of the volunteers, all attempts to get her up failed. Roland feared she had "had enough" and called their vet out. The vet confirmed his worst fears, that due to her age it would be best to put her to sleep. So Dolly ended her days in a nice warm stable, with those she loved around her while she passed over peacefully. We hope she is now with her friends who have passed over the years, at Rainbow Bridge.

GISELLE: OUR GRAND OLD LADY

Giselle, or Jess as we call her, was born in a paddock, on a stormy night, on May 12th, 1975. Her owner, Gerry, named her Giselle, after a ballet which was being performed in a Torquay theatre at the time. Ladybird, Giselle's mum, was immediately led in from the fields by Gerry, who also carried the tiny foal in her arms, wrapped in a blanket, into a warm, dry stable. The little foal, which was struggling to get to its' feet to feed from her mother, was wiped down with a warm towel and Gerry stood back proudly to watch the bonding process.

Gerry told me that Ladybird was a Skewbald, brown patches on white, a New Forest mare of "uncertain temperament, but with a fantastic turn of speed." Giselle's father had a superb, placid temperament and was a stocky bay, pure bred Arab, called Rozak's Star.

Arab[14] or Arabian horses originate from the Arabian Peninsula. Due to an Arabs distinctive head shape, they have refined wedge shaped heads, large eyes, large nostrils, broad foreheads but small muzzles, the way they hold their tails high and their arched necks, they are easy to recognise. Arabs are one of the oldest breeds of horses, dating back some 4,500 years. Over the centuries, these horses have been spread around the world as a result of war and trading. They are bred with other breeds, to improve speed, endurance and refinement. Not surprisingly, Arab blood lines are found in almost every breed of riding horses. Arabs are famous for being good natured, willing to please their owners and quick to learn. However, riders of Arab horses need to be alert, because these horses are also highly strung and very high spirited.

As a yearling, Giselle ran with the farms other young horses, but unexpectedly got herself into trouble – who would have thought it of the cranky old lady we at the sanctuary came to know and love! The result of her liaisons was a little bay colt, which was named William, who ultimately ended up with a family in Berkshire and apparently did well in the Pony Club there.

---

[14] Wikipedia

The whole process of giving birth at a young age and bringing up a little colt the wrong side of the blanket meant that Giselle's growth was restricted. During that time, she was not big enough for her owner to ride but when she got a little older, she took to being ridden so easily, she did not need to be broken in.

Jess was never keen on jumping, but did well in local gymkhanas, winning countless rosettes and teaching her young riders the ropes. Later, she was put out on loan to carefully selected families and was once sold to an old school friend of Gerry's for her daughters to ride. However, as Gerry was keen not to lose touch with Jess, the two friends agreed that when the children had outgrown Jess, she would be returned to Gerry, which is exactly what happened.

When Jess was in her late twenties, Gerry wanted to find her a semi-retirement home and asked the owners of the Devon Horse and Pony Sanctuary if they could take Jess. She arrived at our sanctuary, aged twenty eight, on 5th February 2004.

Jess was later loaned out to a 'Pony School' for young children, at Uphempston, near Totnes. This was run by a lady called Rose Boon. At that time, Rose had several horses on loan from the Devon Horse and Pony Sanctuary, so Sylvia was confident she had recommended a safe home for Jess. Apparently Jess flourished there so she hoped she had found her a home for life.

Unfortunately, around ten years later, Rose decided to move away. Once again, Jess's owner was looking for a permanent home for her. Luckily Roland, who had by that time taken over the ownership of the Devon Horse and Pony Sanctuary from his mother Sylvia, stepped in and gave Jess a permanent home with us. So, at the grand old age of 39, she returned to the sanctuary in early 2014.

Her hand over documents include comments like: 'She has been ridden once a week'. 'When stabled at night, she sometimes kicks the walls. She has done this all her life.' 'She was loved by a lot of children, now adults, who still come and see her' and 'She has come through the winter well considering her age and we think she looks wonderful.'

When we looked back at the photo's Jess's owner provided, it gave us such a thrill to see the old horse we knew and loved, looking very young and alert at various stages in her life. She is showing her age now physically, being a little ragged and grouchy but we could see by the photos how she looked in her prime. I was not surprised to learn she was part Arab. Even at her ripe old age, if she set her mind to go somewhere, she was pretty un-stoppable. She had a firm will.

My partner, Terrina, giving Jess a good brush back in 2014.

I was there on the day Jess was returned to us in 2014. We decided that she would do well in with our other two oldies, so she was put in with Robin and Bella. Diary entries at this time recorded that since Jess arrived back with us, she had visits from her previous owners at the riding stables during January through to March 2014. Sadly, these visits tapered off, when her visitors became distressed by the number of horses we had lost to either old age or ill health in the beginning of that year. However, Gerry, her first owner, never lost touch with us, as she was very keen to follow Jess's life with us and continues to send regular donations to this day.

One thing I found alarming about Jess, when she first arrived, was the donkey style loud braying sound she made when she was annoyed. This usually happened when she was eating and one of her friends came too close. They were treated to this ear-splitting noise and had to get out of her way very quickly, to avoid her back legs as she kicked out at them. She also made this noise when 'talking' to other horses over the fence. It always made me jump out of my skin, the noise was so loud.

She displayed a soft, maternal side to her when Snoopy, an eight month old Welsh Cobb colt arrived with us. You will read in his chapter in this book, that he was abandoned by (we think) gypsies in Cardiff city centre in the middle of the night. On his arrival at our sanctuary, he was stabled to settle him in, but he was terrified of everything and used to career round this confined space if anyone so much as looked over the door.

Jess was in a paddock which was close to the stables and she began to show an interest in Snoopy. Sian decided she would put Jess in the stable next to Snoopy overnight, to keep him company. Jess was very gentle with him and mothered him. When Snoopy was more settled, he was allowed out in the paddock next to Jess during the day and very soon a bond developed between them.

Jess celebrated her 40th birthday with us on Tuesday 12th May, 2015. As she received a lot of attention on a daily basis, it was hard to try and think of something to mark the occasion, other than her usual grooming and perhaps a few more grated apples and carrots in her feed. Julie, one of our volunteers who had taken a shine to Jess, decided to buy her a present, in the form of a brand new summer rug.

Jess had a pretty un-eventful time at the sanctuary. She was rugged up all through the winters and also had a light 'turn out' rug on in the summer, if the weather became cold and too wet. When the weather was dry and sunny, her rug was taken off and she was groomed and she enjoyed soaking up the sun. We also used to apply cream to parts of her because as she grew older, she became rather bony and developed sores easily from being rugged. Putting a fleecy rug under her horse rug to try and stop sores forming did not work as she somehow managed to get that off.

Jess did not have a good history with rugs and got through them at an alarming rate. The birthday rug is long gone, as are the other two she was bought. Once, when she was stabled for some reason, I peered over the top of the stable to see her rug was off and on the floor of the stable, with all the catches still done up. She truly was the master of escapology!

On one occasion, I arrived at the sanctuary to find that somehow, she had got all of her rug around her neck, with the girth straps still done up. The two smaller straps which are supposed to be clipped around her back legs were also still fastened, but her legs were not in them.

Fortunately, she was in one of her better moods that day and allowed me to catch her and re-fit the rug. Some days, it used to take two people to catch her and get the rug back on properly. Still obstinate in her very old age.

During the opening months of 2016, Jess was sometimes found lying down on the floor in her paddock when we arrived at the sanctuary in the mornings. This sight used to make me feel sick with fear, as I thought she was dead. However, often she would be fast asleep and was startled when we called her name; sometimes she would get up straight away but on other occasions, she had to be helped up.

We were all quite worried about her, but as she was eating very well and the warmer weather was on the way, the decision was made to allow her to age gracefully. She was stabled during really cold periods before we left in the afternoons. However, as her dislike of being stabled never changed, she voiced her disapproval noisily and took her frustration out by kicking the stable walls.

As the year progressed, Jess's health began to fluctuate. She was becoming a bit wobbly on her feet and her eyes looked a bit droopy. However, she continued to eat really well and on some days was positively spritely, sometimes being difficult to catch when her rug needed altering or straps needed doing up.

As the colder weather approached, Julie suggested we made up Jess's feed with hot water. Bryan got the old generator repaired, but it took a bit of starting and just because it started, did not mean it wouldn't conk out after a few minutes if you got the choke setting wrong.

This old generator was a temperamental piece of machinery, which I thought should have been in the British Museum and would have driven a saint to swear. There were a number of levers and switches which needed to be in the right place before a cord had to be yanked out, to enable it to start. You then needed to let it run before switching the kettle on. Then, on most occasions, this small load inevitably caused the cantankerous thing to cut out, resulting in blue air in the barn. Angie became a dab hand at keeping this heap going, so this became one of her jobs and she did it very well.

I think getting to grips with the process of starting up the generator, was a bit much for Sian, so on her watch, the oldies had cold food. Eventually, we all tired of trying to run this old machine, so Julie and I started bringing up large flasks of hot water. We felt we wasted too much time and energy getting this old machine not just started, but keeping it running.

By the end of the year, we were concerned about whether Jess would be able to stand another winter. We began to discuss whether we should have her put to sleep before the winter or let her carry on and see how she went. I was now in conversation with her owner Gerry, to keep her informed of Jess's failing health and to make sure she was comfortable with our decision process. Luckily, she understood the very difficult decision ahead of us and gave us her full support in whatever we decided to do.

Those of you who have had animals and who have had to make this terrible decision, will know what a see-saw of emotions we all went through. At what stage do you decide to let an animal go, who is much loved and who appears to be enjoying life? Looking at her trotting about on a lovely sunny, mild day, we felt guilty for even thinking of ending her life.

On the other hand, we felt if we left it too late, she might pass alone, at night in the cold. With the onset of winter, worse weather was on the cards in the next few months and none of us wanted that ending for her.

The decision as to when to call the vet was taken out of our hands, because the number of times she was found 'down' in the mornings increased. It was also becoming more and more difficult to get Jess up. Although Jess was old and skinny, she was still a big horse and weighed a lot. Getting her up involved trying three things. Plan A involved pushing her rear backwards and forwards in a rocking motion to try and get her to stand. That never worked. If she was on a slope, plan B was for the two of us to get hold of her front and back feet and try and roll her right over, so she was facing downhill, in the hopes this would help. Ropes were needed for this, so we had to be quick, because when she did get up, we had to get these off before she tripped over them. Plan C was to put a lead reign on her and try and pull her up. My chiropractor made quite a bit of money out of me during this period.

The time came, when we knew we had to stop skirting round the issues. I called a meeting between us all to discuss and agree not *whether* to put her to sleep, but *when*. We were divided. Sian and I wanted to allow her to pass gracefully, but Julie and Bryan were keen to try and keep her going a while longer.

Following these heart rending discussions about when to do the deed, an agreement was reached that she would be put to sleep the following week, when the owners of the sanctuary were on site, to help and give us all moral support. Julie and Bryan were still worried whether we were doing the right thing, so they arranged for Karen the horse whisperer, who had worked with little Humphrey and Fie, to come in and "talk" to Jess.

Jess pretty much told Karen what we all knew in our heart of hearts – she had had enough and wanted to 'go'. She told Karen she wanted to pass over with those she loved around her, on a sunny day, in the top paddock where she could see her favourite view.

She also told Karen that there was a 'big black horse waiting with her, to help her pass over.' This had to be Captain, our massive black horse who had passed away some years earlier. At the time of Karen's visit; Jess was in his old paddock. For those sceptics amongst you, Karen knew nothing of Captain. Jess also said that she struggled to eat her present diet of nuts, chaff and mix. It was all a bit hard on her gums and the few teeth she had left, so she asked for different food and for that to be soaked overnight and could we continue to put some hot water over it?

Julie and Bryan immediately went out and bought her mash and grass nuts. This food was soaked overnight to soften and each morning, warm water from our flasks was poured over the food for the three oldies, Jess, Robin and Bella, so they could all enjoy a hot meal. I have never seen the three of them gobble up their food so fast and enjoy a second hot feed later in the day, just before we left. The new food seemed to give Jess a new strength, which was wonderful, but at the same time, re-fuelled our worries as to whether we were planning to put her to sleep too soon.

We all loved Jess very much, but we were mindful that the weather was quickly becoming very cold and icy. Jess really did 'want to go' and no one wanted to come up to the sanctuary to find her either dead in the morning or half dead, lying in the cold. Jess was our oldest resident – she had led a lovely life and we wanted her to end it the way she wanted and with the dignity and comfort she deserved.

Less than a week after Karen's visit, Jess was put to sleep on the morning of 17th February, 2017; with all of us around her. It was the day we had all been dreading, but we took comfort in the fact it was a nice sunny, if not cold day. Julie, Bryan and I had worked hard to finish all the chores during the time we were waiting for Roland, Alison and the vet to turn up. We kept reassuring each other that we were doing the right thing and recounting stories about Jess's life at our sanctuary. Julie had taken Jess's rug off, so we were grooming her and giving her lots of cuddles when Roland, Alison and the vet arrived.

Although we were grateful Kevin was on time, we now had to steel ourselves to say our final goodbyes to Jess. While Kevin prepared the initial sedative injection to make her a bit woozy, we all gathered round Jess to cuddle her and tell her we loved her.

This initial injection did indeed make her a bit woozy, but she did not go down to the floor as anticipated. It took four of us to steady her as she began to sway, but she steadfastly refused to go down. Stubborn to the end, bless her, Kevin warned us to stand clear as he had no choice but to administer the final, lethal injection, while she was still on her feet.

On all the other occasions I have had to witness a horse being put to sleep, they have been laying down, so I found this all a bit stressful. However, within seconds of this injection being administered, she started to slide down to the ground very gracefully. As she did, Kevin asked all of us to move in quickly to her, so we could support her head. She slipped away very quickly. She was probably dead before she hit the floor. All you could hear in our yard were the sounds of Julie and I sobbing and whispering words of love for our beloved Jess.

As I knelt over Jess and stroked her head, I sent up a silent prayer that Captain was indeed waiting for her, to help her transition to the other side. I hoped that she would be happy to be free of her old body and join past companions from the sanctuary, who we hoped would also be waiting to welcome her at Rainbow Bridge.

Although we all knew the right decision had been made for her, it was a tough one to come to terms with, even as we looked down at her tired, old bony body. She would be sorely missed, she was a character right up to the end. The only horse I ever knew, who could get out of a horse rug with all the straps still done up. Rest in peace dear Jess, you deserved your dignified end.

We opened the gate between Jess's body and the paddock that Robin and Bella were in. I was taken aback, but really pleased, to see them come up immediately and sniff at Jess's body. When they had said their goodbyes, we covered her body with a few horse rugs whilst we waited for the Cremtor lorry to arrive and take her away.

As always, I could not witness the sight of the body of one of our beloved horses being winched into the back of their lorry. I hid in the barn and took the opportunity to have a gut wrenching cry in private. The people who cremate the horses made some bracelets for us from Jess's hair. Julie and I wear ours all the time and appreciate such a memento, a memory of our beloved Jess's time with us.

VERA (COME INTO MY PADDOCK IF YOU THINK YOU ARE HARD ENOUGH) AND HOLLY.

Vera, a small black horse, arrived at the sanctuary on 26th February 2011. Little is known of her history, except she was owned by a local farmer who wanted to shoot her and have her butchered for meat. His wife did not want to see her shot, so she contacted Roland and asked if he could take her. When Vera had been collected, she told her husband the horse had 'disappeared'. When Vera arrived with us, she joined the other horses at Southcott.

On arrival, she was stabled next to Dolly, as the girls planned to put her in a paddock with Dolly and Comic. The girls referred to Vera as 'the yearling' and as they knew she had not had a head collar on yet, she was left to settle in for a couple of days and get used to her surroundings, before the girls started working on her.

Micala's diary entry for the day after Vera's arrival, gave the girls a flavour of what was to come and what they could expect from this horse: "*Vera! Yearling will kick (*heavily underlined) *be careful. You can scratch her withers,* (shoulders to you and me) *but do not let her be bossy. Don't let her out with Miranda, she'll kick her. She seems ok with Robin and Lucky*."

By early March, as well as continuing to be aggressive, Vera added escaping into other paddocks to her repertoire. However, despite her unreliable temperament, the girls were making progress with her. They managed to get a head collar on her and were able to lead her out of her paddock into the yard, to eat her food. The girls were sensibly still very wary of her and were very cautious when trying to get her used to her legs being touched.

Vera was moved around quite a bit during her early days at the sanctuary. The girls were trying to find horses she would get on well with, without her dominating them, which was proving difficult. In addition to this, some of our horses had already formed very strong attachments with each other, so the girls were reticent to move horses away from their friends, to enable them to match Vera with those she got on well with. She was put in a paddock with Dolly, Lewis and Comic. The girls felt as Lewis was possessive over Dolly and this made Comic sulk (I am not sure how you can tell when a horse is sulking) they thought Vera might add a welcome distraction into the mix. However, a few days later, the girls noticed that Vera and Dolly were not getting on very well, which resulted in poor Dolly getting kicked, so the girls had no choice but to move Vera into another paddock.

Vera continued to be a bit of a problem in this respect, but the girls persevered over the weeks and months which followed, until they found horses she was calmer with. She settled in and appeared to calm down a little and there were bigger gaps between her being good and those when we had to rush to get behind a wheel barrow, or up a hedge when she charged us. There were many warnings in the diary about Vera. Most of the warnings centred on the fact she was bad tempered, so we were all told to watch her back end. If she was displeased, her ears would flatten and she would swing round and lash out with her back legs. I think calling Vera "a bit nutty" was a massive understatement. In my opinion, at that time, she was a psychopath, you never know what sort of mood she would be in. When I first started to go up to the sanctuary, one of the first things I was told was to be careful around her. All new volunteers receive the same warning.

By early April, the girls were able to groom Vera, as long as she was tied up. A diary entry for April 2011, states: "Vera brushed and messed about with. She is coming on well with her legs now." I presume that meant she was not using them with intent to harm. I thought the girls were very brave to persevere with her.

As time went on the girls continued to work on handling Vera and she became accepting and used to their attention. It was good preparation in case we were lucky enough to find someone special who was willing to take this head-case on and offer her a loan home. The girls were also working up to leading her down the small lanes to the village. By early June, Vera was comfortable with being groomed, her feet being picked out and she was allowing the girls to put a bridle on her. As the girls are all still all alive, one presumes Vera remained happy with what they were doing.

Come on in, if you think you are hard enough...the Vera stare.

I did not join in any of the handling Vera was receiving at this time as I did not consider myself brave enough. However, you will read how she progressed over the years at the end of this chapter.

In September 2011, I was mentioned specifically in the diary, but not for a good reason. The girls said that Vera was getting even more bolshie. They decided (quite rightly) it was because I used to take carrots up and feed them to all the horses. However, in Vera's paddock, these treats were now banned, because it made her even more aggressive. She did not like the other horses getting these treats and would go to great lengths to chase these creatures away. The girls said that even though they never took carrots or any treats in to Vera's paddock, she assumed they did, because I did and she became aggressive and pushy with them. I am not sure how I didn't work that out for myself.

Vera being pushy and aggressive is not the sort of thing you want to be anywhere near. From that time on, no one went in her paddock, unless they had a wheel barrow to put between them and her. I was in trouble for exacerbating her aggression, which was fair enough.

I was relieved about this ban, as I had had more than one lucky escape which was as a result of my giving Vera and her companions' carrots. While Vera was out of the way busy hoovering hers up from the floor, I had walked over to her companions, Herbie and Haidi and started to feed them.

Suddenly, the sound of thundering hooves behind me made me spin round and I was horrified to see Vera coming at me and my dog Milo at full throttle. Even though she is not a big horse, she looked very intimidating. I was sure her ears were not flat on her head for aerodynamic, speed enhancing reasons. I screamed at Milo to run and put the wheel barrow I was using to poo pick, between me and her. I threw some carrots down on the floor to distract her and walked very quickly in the other direction, carefully keeping the wheel barrow between us.

In the weeks and months that followed, even though I no longer took carrots or any other treats in to her paddock, Vera continued to follow me around. This was not a casual walk behind me, but constantly barging me and then finally, when she realised I had no carrots, expressing her frustration by spinning round and lashing out with her hind legs. Luckily, my trusty wheel barrow was always between us, ready for these bouts of her bad temper, so I was safe. I always kept a wary eye on her whilst poo picking, which was just as well, because one day she galloped all the way over from the other side of the paddock just for the thrill of charging me. I had to jump up on the hedge to avoid her as the wheelbarrow was not close enough to hide behind. Better to be a coward all in one piece, than be brave and in casualty. I still looked round, however, just to make sure a passing walker had not witnessed my shameful cowardice.

In September, 2011, Vera tried to bite Micala's daughter, so this prompted the girls to discuss what to do with this "stroppy horse." The girls decided they only had two options (i) re-home her, or (ii) try to break her in themselves. They quite rightly put her aggression down to boredom. During October, when one of the girls was touching Vera's front legs, (bravely in my opinion) to get her used to being handled – she was kicked. Despite this, the girls recorded in the diary that "Vera is making progress!" Really? Progress in picking us off, one by one?

Early on in March 2012, Vera aimed a vicious kick at Sian. Luckily, it caught the wheel barrow she also used as a shield when in Vera's paddock and not Sian's leg. Sian wrote in our diary: "She meant it, so be warned".

We have had quite a few failed re-homing attempts with Vera over the years. The first time Vera went out on loan, she kicked the owners (valuable) horse and we were nearly sued. Roland and Alison were told to "come and pick her up immediately". The second time she went out on loan, she kicked and bit a small child so she was back with us a lot faster than she came in. Fair enough. Sadly, during the years which followed, although we have made attempts to home her, Vera always comes back.

At the end of 2014, Sian found Vera laying down in her field and as she could not get her up, she called out the emergency vet, who diagnosed 'Mild Colic.' Vera had to be stabled so we could keep an eye on her for a few days. Karen (my friend and a volunteer up there at that time) decided she was confident to lead Vera from her paddock, up to the stables. Karen successfully got a lead reign on Vera and led her towards the gate, but as she stopped to open this, Vera lashed out with one of her front legs and delivered an excruciatingly painful blow to the area just above Karen's knee.

Poor Karen was in agonies, but bravely hobbled up through the next few paddocks to the stables. If Vera's kick had landed a few inches further down, a new knee cap might have been in order. Who knows what motivated Vera's vicious attack. Maybe fear of what was happening, maybe she was in pain, or maybe just in a bad mood. Following a few days in a stable with Bute powder in her food, Vera was returned to her paddock, back to terrorising her companions. Karen left it to Sian to take Vera back to her paddock.

In June 2016; we were lucky to find a loan home for Vera and her still in one piece mate Holly, a white spotted miniature Shetland. This House and Gardens, open to the public, was just a few miles up the road and had agreed to give them both a home. We all felt this was an ideal home for our Vera, as she would be out in their paddocks with quite a lot of human contact, but with the 'visitors' on the other, safer side of the fence. We had high hopes that this might turn out to be Vera's 'forever home'. There were no other horses she could attack or children she could bite.

Perhaps I should explain here, what happens when one of our horses goes 'out on loan'. As a charity, we do not sell our horses on, because we would never be able to keep track of where they are and whether they are being well cared for and are still enjoying a good life.

So, anyone who is interested in giving one of our horses a loan home, has to have their property inspected to ensure they have the necessary infrastructure for the horse and we talk to them to find out if they are experienced in horse management. They then have to sign a contract which details their responsibilities. These include ensuring if the horse falls ill, it must be seen by a vet, the horse must be seen by a farrier regularly and the person must pay all the bills. The loan owner has to ensure the horse is well fed and foot the bills for this as well.

The contract is also meant to prevent the horse being sold or loaned to anyone else. If the person who signs the contract no longer wants to keep the horse, it must be returned to us. We do regular home checks to ensure the horse is being looked after. If we are at all concerned, it comes back to us.

Sometimes, a person who takes one of our horses out on loan has a change in circumstances. They may become ill, suffer from long term health problems or move to a smaller place – any of which results in them not being able to care for the horse. Unfortunately, the former applied in Vera and Holly's case. A year after they had left us, Roland was contacted by the owners of the country house, one of whom had become unwell. They told him they did not feel they were able to look after Vera and Holly any more.

Roland brought Vera and Holly back to our sanctuary in early June, 2017 and said they "need feeding up." He put them in our bottom paddock while the girls decided where they might be placed. The girls decided that Vera and Holly would be put in a lower paddock, until they settled in. I was not particularly comfortable with this decision, because I felt Vera would benefit from more company, but I could see the logic behind the girl's decision.

Kelly and Lara, our new members of staff, had been told all about how Vera could be a little un-predictable and they were rightly concerned for their safety and the safety of their young children. These children had been coming up at weekends for around a month prior to Vera's return and were grooming a lot of the horses. Given Vera's previous record of biting children and charging at people and dogs, it was felt until everyone got used to her and vice versa, it would be better all-round if she was in a paddock no one had to cross to get to other horses. There is, after all, a limit to how many people, children and dogs we could get behind one small wheel barrow.

On the day Vera arrived 'home', she was in very high spirits. The next day, she was still very excited and as she had somehow gotten her head collar off over night, Kelly and Lara had their work cut out trying to get her through two paddocks to where they wanted to keep her. All attempts failed to get a head collar back on her, so one was put on Holly with the idea that Vera might follow her down. Vera did follow Holly down through the paddocks, but only after she had run round each of them, loudly trumpeting her return. All this noisy galloping around, bucking and kicking probably filled some of our horses with dread that she was back. They were certainly very unsettled while all this was going on. They weren't the only ones.

A few weeks after Vera was put into her new paddock, which in the past we had seldom used, we noticed the skin on her chest and neck was raw. In addition to this, both she and Holly were being plagued with flies. On investigation, we found there was a boggy area a short distance from our boundary fence and this was attracting masses of flies, the majority of which seemed to be making a bee-line for poor Vera.

It was with some trepidation on my arrival on Wednesday, I read in the diary that I had to take some soothing Aloe Vera gel down to her paddock to try and get some on her. I was shocked, but pleased, when she allowed me to not only get close to her, but that I came away unscathed after rubbing cooling gel on the affected areas on her face, neck and back.

As the days went by, we were all growing more concerned about the effect the flies were having on Vera. Lara and I decided it would be best to move Vera and Holly up a few paddocks, away from the boggy area and to one where there was a shelter. We knew this would solve the fly problem, as the horses would be able to shelter in the shade to get away from them. This move had the added benefit that Vera would be next to her old mates and we wouldn't be bitten badly by the flies, whilst we were in her paddock.

We discussed the logistics of this move, as there were several alternatives. The first option was to get them out of the top gate, but there were horses in the paddock the other side – so we would have to move them up to their shelter and shut them in while we moved Vera and Holly. The paddock was a really big one, so to get Vera and Holly across to their new paddock, we would have to rope some of it off, to stop them grazing or worse, running around that massive space. It would have taken us longer to prepare than it would have to actually herd them into the new paddock.

We then discussed and agreed an alternative solution that we thought would be less labour intensive and therefore quicker. There was a second, metal gate at the far side of Vera's paddock, which led out into a small boggy area. The paddock we wanted Vera and Holly to go in was to the left and was accessed via a very old wooden gate about fifty yards into that area on the left hand side. I suggested we should rope off a corridor between both gates, along the side of a wall and then open the old wooden gate which led into their new paddock. Then open their metal gate to let them out of their paddock and they would walk along this corridor, go into the new paddock and all we had to do was shut the old wooden gate behind them. Less preparation. Job done. Or so we thought.

Lara and I opened the wooden gate which led into the new paddock from said boggy area and we began to rope off a wide corridor between the two gates, for Vera and Holly to come through. By this time, Vera and Holly were at their metal gate, watching what we were doing. We had roped off only a few feet from the wooden gate, when Lara shouted out: "Holly is coming through". I spun round, just in time to see Holly force her way through the fencing by the side of their metal gate and come hurtling towards me. She was clearly very desperate to get out of her fly infested paddock.

I was horrified. I was worried that as we had not finished roping the area off, she would run the wrong way and get stuck in the bog. In that split second, I wondered if my idea was going to lead to disaster. Too late now. Holly abruptly slowed down and turned away from the bog and calmly trotted past me, into the new paddock. My relief was very short lived, when I realised what was going to happen next.

Vera, either in a panic because Holly had disappeared, or just desperate to get out of her old paddock, was literally throwing herself against the metal gate, which Lara had not had a chance to open. She had to now. Luckily, it opened outwards towards Lara and as she found the strength to wrench it open, fighting the brambles which had grown around it undisturbed for many years – Vera came crashing through. Headed straight for me.

Her ears were back and she was snorting with both fear and anger. She suddenly stopped, turned and ran straight into the boggy area. Lara urged me to be quiet and not make eye contact – she hoped Vera would calm down and work out which way to get into her new paddock. Vera stopped, turned back towards me and cantered over. Fighting the urge to bolt up the stone wall, I held my ground, holding on to what little rope I had put up and opening my arms to try and block her going the wrong way.

She went past me, toward the open wooden gate, but stopped a few feet away from me. I was determined to close the space around her, but didn't want to wave the rope at her rear, in case it spooked her and she ran away from the gate, or worse still, kicked me. Just as she started to move forward, towards the open gate, she changed her mind and suddenly whirled round and faced me.

To say I was scared is a bit of an understatement, but slowly, I walked towards her, holding my arms out wide, still hanging on to the one piece of rope I had, which might stop her going to the right, back into the bog. Suddenly, she turned and galloped into her new paddock, with me in hot pursuit, frantically dragging the old wooden gate closed before she changed her mind and charged back to us.

Lara and I were mentally and physically exhausted. Sweaty with exertion and a bit of fear thrown in, we moved towards each other, put our hands in the air and gave each other a 'high five'. Our plans had not gone as smoothly as we had wished, but Vera and Holly were charging round their new paddock and none of us were injured. We checked Holly on our way back up through their paddock to the yard, but amazingly, she didn't have a scratch on her after her emergency exit from the old paddock through the fencing. By the time we reached the top of their paddock, Vera was already in her shelter. No more horses were ever allowed back in that lower paddock.

Early in June, 2017, Roland thought he had found a home for Holly. As this was "in the wilds of Hampshire" and too far away for any of us to go and do a home check; he enlisted the help of a very well-known national animal rescue charity to go and visit this prospective home. They reported back that they felt certain this home would be suitable.

So, trusting their judgement (and why wouldn't you?) Roland brought his horse box down to the sanctuary and although Holly had been easy to catch, getting her in the box was totally another matter. It took him, me and Alison a good hour to entice Holly in but each time we got her in, she bolted out of the side door. In the end, we got her up the ramp by enticing her in with a bowl of food, Roland shut the ramp and I shot out of the side door as Alison slammed it shut.

It took Roland and Alison the rest of the day to get to this place in Hampshire. However, when they arrived at what was to be Holly's new home, one look out of the window of their car told them they had had a wasted journey. It was right next to a Shetland stud farm, with little or no fencing to protect the animals in the fields next door, which were owned by the man who was offering Holly a new home.

Roland and Alison carried out a thorough inspection of the rest of the property, together with the other animals in this man's care. As a result, Roland and Alison were on their way back to Devon very quickly. For me, it says a lot about their dedication to our horses and their welfare that they were not prepared to leave Holly there even overnight while they found somewhere to rest before setting off the next day back to Devon. They began the long journey back immediately and reached our Devon sanctuary well after dark.

Poor Holly, exhausted and stressed, was put into a stable with clean bedding, food and water before the also exhausted and stressed Roland and Alison left the sanctuary. The next day, Holly was re-united with her mate Vera.

Our horses are moved around regularly, to allow paddocks to rest and for the horses to have access to better grass. Vera was no exception and it was for this reason she found herself in one quite close to our yard. She appeared to have settled down and mellowed out, so all of us up there were comfortable with either being in her paddock or crossing it. However, one weekend late in July, only a month after she had been returned to us, she bit Kelly's younger son. It was completely un-provoked. As a result of this, Kelly and I immediately moved Vera and Holly down a paddock, so the children had less contact with this nutcase.

There were no more recorded incidents of Vera doing anyone any more damage during the remaining months of 2017, although Sian did note early in August that: "Vera in a foul mood." Late in September, Kelly noticed Vera eating the acorns which had dropped from the two huge trees in her paddock. She had read they are poisonous to eat when green, so immediately roped off the areas where the acorns had dropped. There was no damage done and Roland said Vera would be fine.

Vera remained on fine form, chasing Angie's dog, Toby, as we poo picked her area. Angie had joined as a volunteer, as you will have read in previous chapters of this book. Milo had long since learnt not to go in Vera's paddock. Sian recorded in the diary late November that Vera was "in a very bad mood and charged at me today." In December, Sian also recorded that: "Vera in a funny mood" and the next day Vera was "being a right bitch."

At the time of writing, both Vera and Holly are still at the sanctuary. However, following Micala's return to the sanctuary early in 2018, she made it her mission to ensure all horses were handled daily and this included the lovely Vera. Micala has a fantastic way with horses and had no trouble at all, getting a head collar on Vera first time. She made sure that each day Vera was groomed and Micala got her used to having her feet lifted each day, progressing to having her feet picked out as well. I have been amazed at the change in Vera.

During my time at the sanctuary, all attempts to get Vera's feet trimmed by a farrier have resulted in failure. During one attempt, Vera reared up and kicked out at the person hanging on to her (me) and on a subsequent visit, a farrier received a nasty bite on his rear. No one can blame a farrier for not wanting to get injured and in any case, it proved impossible to get Vera anywhere near them.

Micala, however, was not to be beaten. In June 2018, following another disastrous attempt to get Vera's feet done, she took the decision to seek Roland's permission to sedate Vera for the next farriers visit; which he duly gave. Joy (our new member of staff, who joined in June 2018) caught Vera and the sedative was administered but this only made her marginally calmer. The farrier (probably fearing for his life again) gave up pretty quickly trying to get Vera to lift her feet, but Joy bravely persevered and within fifteen minutes had got one of Vera's legs up. Vera didn't, however, tolerate the farrier working on her feet, but he said due to the breed of horse she was, he was not concerned about the fact her feet had not been done for years, but encouraged Joy to work on her for his next visit. I am delighted to report that thanks to Joy and Micala's persistence, Vera is now seen by the farrier regularly.

Micala helped my confidence so much, that I was able to pluck up the courage to put a head collar on Vera and lead her in and out of the yard and stable for her feeds. The daily handling has given her an interest and reduced her boredom, which in turn has reduced her aggression and calmed her down.

Another major breakthrough was yet to come. Joy made it her mission to start lunging Vera with an end goal of breaking her in. Vera now accepts a bridle and seems to enjoy these sessions. Unfortunately, the winter weather stopped progress late in 2018, but Joy plans to break Vera in this year. I live in hope that one day, we might find this clever, but bored and sometimes unpredictable horse a 'forever home'. If not, at least Vera is getting the attention she so badly needs.

SNOOPY: ABANDONED BY GYPSIES IN CARDIFF CITY CENTRE WHEN HE WAS TWO MONTHS OLD.

Roland and Alison receive many calls each week, begging them to take in neglected or abandoned horses and the decisions they have to make are hard ones. Which ones to take and which ones to say no to? There is no specific criteria; maybe it is the story behind the horse, or maybe, it is whether we can squeeze another one in. In this particular case, it was a combination of the fact we had the space, the horse's abandonment story and the fact we had recently lost another young Welsh Cob, Humphrey, recently and they wanted us to be able to care for and succeed with this one.

We had been told by Roland that Cardiff City Council in Wales had rescued a little foal, found wandering around Cardiff city centre late at night, terrified. They immediately contacted a local horse sanctuary, who came out and collected the little chap. Unfortunately, they were unable to keep the foal permanently, as they were at maximum capacity, so they rang Roland who agreed to take him.

Snoopy, as Sian named him, arrived with us on 12th August 2014, after a period of quarantine in Wales. The paper work which accompanied Snoopy estimated that he was born somewhere around 1st May 2014, as his rescuers thought he was only a few months old when he suffered this terrible ordeal.

On his arrival, Snoopy was stabled. Even at his tender young age, he was un-approachable and used to dash round his stable in a panic when we attempted to go in with him. Within a few days Sian decided that as Snoopy was terrified of people, it would be a good idea to put an older, quiet horse in the stable next to him. She chose Jess, our eldest resident and they quickly bonded.

At that time, the stables in each block were separated by gates, so the two horses could see each other. Sian also recommended that our contact with Snoopy was very quiet with slow movements, so as not to panic or scare him. She asked that we went in the stable and sit with him, to try and get him used to people. We were not to try and touch him, just sit there and let him get used to us.

However, as I was only at the sanctuary a few days a week, poor Snoopy did not know me as he did Sian. When I tried to go in with him to give him his feed of a section of soaked hay in his rack and a quarter of a scoop of Alfa, a quarter scoop of soaked foal nuts, the poor little creature bolted round the stable terrified. Whilst I knew I should stay in there with him, my attempts to calm him did not work, so I left the food and shut the door.

A week after his arrival, thanks to Sian's daily perseverance, she was able to start Snoopy's worm treatment. By the end of August, Snoopy was finding his feet and the diary entry for 24th states: "Snoopy a monster." By mid-September, Snoopy was given the run of our yard and within a few days, the gate was opened to a small paddock for a few hours a day, so he could get some exercise and still feel secure. By the first week in October, he had the run of the bottom paddock as well. He was growing fast and was very excitable, loving the space to charge around in.

At the end of October, he was let out into a larger paddock and it was great to see him rocket out of his stable, kicking his back legs out with the sheer joy of being let out. He now trusted Sian enough to let her put a head collar on him and groom him for a short while.

The only problem we had with Snoopy was that he had had no one to teach him any manners. So Sian decided that he needed to go in with a few other horses, so they could teach him the rules. He was put in with Pippin and later, when he arrived with us, Buster joined the two of them.

When he was younger, I did my best with Snoopy, making a fuss of him, but later, when he was out in the paddocks, he would always put his ears back when he saw me approaching. I always had a bad feeling about him and maybe he sensed this, because as he grew bigger, he did become quite aggressive towards me, wasting no time at all in trying to take a chunk out of my hand or arm.

I found trying to get across his paddock with food for horses in the next field, was quite an ordeal and I lost count of the times I used the wheel barrow as a shield as he came rocketing towards me at full pelt, then crowded me when I tried to keep him away from the food bowls. Roland recommended I tried pushing him away, as this normally worked, but in Snoopy's case, this only resulted in him flattening his ears and spinning round, in preparation for a kick from his back legs.

My jumping up and down and waving my arms around did not have the desired effect of making him respect my space and back off, as it did with the other horses at feed times. Instead, he would turn round and lash out at me with his back legs. I have to admit I ended up being very nervous around him and of course he picked up on that and milked it for all he was worth. I think he used to look forward to Wednesdays. It was his entertainment day, spotting me in his paddock, thundering over to me and seeing how quickly I could run. I thought it was better to be a live coward than a squashed or kicked brave person.

One time, when Snoopy was in a paddock next to Fie, Angie and I plotted long and hard how we might get past him, so we could get in to feed her and her mates. It was decided that Angie would throw carrots over the gate, to distract Snoopy, while I climbed over the wall and into Fie's paddock. Seriously cowardly. Micala, had she been with us then, would not have stood for his behaviour and would have opened the gate to his paddock, pushed him away and walked into Fie's field.

I had five bowls of food to lift on top of the wall and balance there. Then I had to climb up one side and down the other into Fie's paddock and then try and put all the bowls down at a decent distance from each other before the five horses thundered over and began the usual scrap to get their feeds. Bramble, the biggest of the five horses in that paddock was a gentle horse, but like all the others, when there was food about, he was as pushy as the next horse.

Shannon was next in the pecking order and when she and Bramble had decided which of the bowls they would eat from, Fie would come over for hers. As she had supplements in her feed, I used to try and feed her apart from the rest, but at times she wanted to eat out of some of the other bowls and on top of all that, Rudolph and Snowflake were also pushed aside from their bowls, once Shannon had wolfed hers down and homed in on the fact they had not finished theirs. So, all in all, quite a stressful exercise.

Sian appeared not to mind Snoopy's growing aggression, even though even she had been and still was regularly on the receiving end of various bites and attempted kicks. I had broached the subject of him being gelded, but she was adamant that this was not going to happen. She wanted to eventually take him out of the sanctuary on loan and was very against the gelding.

We had already crossed swords regarding Snoopy. I was growing more concerned about his aggression and repeatedly asked her not to put him between me and Fie's paddock, as he made my life very difficult when getting passed him with the other horses food. As she continued to ignore my requests, reluctantly, in the end, I had to ask Roland if he could back me up. Quite rightly, he said that no one up there should be exposed to potential harm, if it could be avoided. He spoke to Sian and she moved Snoopy. Most of the time, she kept him in a paddock I did not have to cross.

I had been told that, apparently, gelding should be carried out before the summer. This was because in the hot weather, flies would be attracted to the wound, increasing the chances of infection. So, my discussions with Sian about getting Snoopy gelded, in the hopes it would calm him down, kicked off again as the warmer weather approached. I had to enlist the help of Roland again, because Sian and I couldn't agree and whilst we had been busy talking about gelding him, Snoopy had bitten Angie. He still continued to show aggression not just to me now, but to the other horses. I needed Roland to pull rank and ask Sian to get the vet in, before one of us or one of our horses was injured. I felt bad going over her head, but to be fair to me, I had tried for some time to reason with her.

On 24th March, 2015, Snoopy was gelded and vaccinated. Sian was not at all happy about this, but the rest of us hoped this might calm him down. He was growing at an alarming rate and was getting very full of himself, so we hoped he would be easier to handle.

Snoopy making friends with Bella.

Snoopy just prior to being broken in. 2017

It took a while, but following the gelding, the attention Sian was giving him and learning lessons from his two companions Pippin and Buster, Snoopy seemed to calm down. Over the following years, Snoopy and I seemed to get along a little better. He still liked to charge over to me, but backed off when I waved my arms around. More often than not, he allowed me to make a fuss of him out in his paddock. I never did quite get up the courage, or trust him enough, to groom him, or to put a head collar on him though.

My feeling of un-ease with him still lingered with me, so I was very relieved when Sian took him out of the sanctuary in 2017 to have him broken in. When this process was complete, she officially took him, out on loan, from where he had been broken, straight back to her paddocks. She enjoyed some wonderful rides on him, until one day, he bucked her off for no apparent reason. She needed urgent medical attention.

PEACHES AND VICTOR: ABANDONED BY GYPSIES.

When Cardiff City Council had contacted Alison and asked her if she could take Snoopy, they also asked her if we could take two small Shetland ponies that had been abandoned and left to fly graze in a back yard somewhere in Cardiff without food and water. Fly grazing is a huge problem in the UK and especially in Wales, where gypsy ponies are left to fend for themselves to feed. They often end up on roads and in places where it is very dangerous for them. Poor Snoopy and Peaches and Victor, as they were later named, were victims of this cruel practice.

It was estimated that these two little ponies had survived for weeks by living on the only food and water they could find, weeds which were growing out of the walls of the back yard and rainwater that collected in small puddles on the concrete.

Peaches and Victor had obviously been handled in their lives as their rescuers had no problems with putting head collars on both of them and leading them from their backyard, into a waiting horse box. These poor ponies were dangerously under nourished and their hooves had grown so much, they had started to turn up at the ends, which made walking very difficult for them.

These two cute Shelties arrived a few weeks after Snoopy, in early September, 2014. They were immediately stabled, fed and wormed. Peaches, the Piebald one and Victor, the slightly bigger Skewbald one both had gypsy plaits in their manes. We were told by the Police and the horse warden that these plaits were a sure sign these horses had been stolen by gypsies. The gypsies normally send someone to scout out horses they want to steal and this scout will plait the manes to identify them and leave. Then the gypsies return later to steal them.

Peaches and Victor were quarantined on arrival at our sanctuary. This is because when we take on rescue cases from areas where Strangles[15] is prevalent, we have to quarantine new arrivals until they have been checked over by a vet and blood tests have been taken. Although these two little ponies had been

[15] Source – British Horse Society Web site.

kept in Wales for a few weeks to ensure they were not exhibiting any signs of Strangles, we could not risk the welfare of our other horses, if these new ones were contaminated.

Strangles is a highly contagious disease which can affect any breed, sex or age of horse. It is spread by direct contact between horses (nose to nose) or indirectly by their owners; such as sharing equipment between horses, such as feeding bowls, water troughs, grooming equipment or saddles and bridles. Unfortunately, signs of the onset of strangles are not normally seen until a period of between three to fourteen days after the horse has been in contact with the bacterium. In this time an infected horse can spread the disease to other horses.

I understand that each case of Strangles is treated on an individual basis by vets, to ensure the appropriate treatment for the horse concerned. Most affected horses recover over a period of a few weeks.

In severe cases, which are thankfully very small, the infection spreads causing abscesses to form in lymph nodes and organs around the body. This condition, which is known as 'bastard strangles' is potentially fatal. An additional complication associated with Strangles causes bleeding into the skin, gums and internal organs and this is also fatal.

You can understand now, why we are so very careful with new arrivals, particularly when they come from an area where Strangles has been known. Kevin came out within a day to examine these two. He would have been looking for clinical signs which would have included loss of appetite, nasal discharge, coughing, high temperature and swelling of the lymph nodes glands. He said he couldn't detect any obvious symptoms for the disease, but he sent off blood tests and took nasal swabs over a period of three weeks, which also test for the bacteria.

Until the blood tests came back and all three swabs were clear, the two new ponies remained stabled and we took extreme precautions to ensure we washed our hands with anti-bacterial spray after touching Peaches and Victor and we did not use their food bowls for any other horse.

The results of the blood tests and swabs came back on the 1st September, showing both horses were clear of Strangles. A week later, after the ponies had been let out into their new paddock;

Kevin was called out again. Peaches had got her head stuck between the gate and the gate post in her paddock and her head was very swollen as a result. She was given Bute for two days and Vaseline was put on her sores.

Perhaps Peaches was a little cross with her experience, because a few weeks later, she bit Sian on the shoulder. We are all sure these two have "little man" syndrome, because whilst Peaches prefers to bite, Victor is known to kick out when he is angry.

Peaches and Victor left the sanctuary in April 2016, to go out on loan to the owners of a small country house, which is open to the public, which is only a few miles up the road from the sanctuary. Sian was able to carry out regular home checks, as she worked there at the time.

Sadly, due to the owner becoming ill, Peaches and Victor were returned to us early in May 2017. Roland and Alison collected Peaches and Victor and walked them back the few miles to the sanctuary. The ponies were a little frightened and on arrival at Southcott, but they were settled in a stable with fresh bedding, food and water. Although at first they stayed nervously at the back of the stable, within a day they were let out into a paddock and as soon as their head collars were taken off, they ran around, kicking up their heels and quickly went to the fence to meet our larger residents in the next paddock. No doubt they were looking forward to getting up to their old tricks of following us round their paddock as we poo picked and pushing the wheel barrow over when it was full.

There is a bit of a mystery around them which no one seems able to clear up. As you will have read, both Peaches and Victor were found abandoned and all evidence pointed to gypsies being the culprits. However, every horse which has to be transported, has to have a passport and these two arrived at our sanctuary with one each. Peaches Passport states, rather grandly, that her name is 'Chapelton Peaches' and that she was born on 22nd May, 2011. Victor's posh name is Coedgleision Victor. Born on 7th May 2011.

No one seems to know the origin of the details on both their passports. There is no way gypsies would have had access to their passports when they stole Peaches and Victor, as one presumes these documents must have been held by their owner. Whoever abandoned them would not have had the passports to leave behind with the horses. So where did these passports come from? The rescuers would not have known their full names and dates of birth.

Victor and Peaches – munching on carrots.

Early in 2018, poor Peaches was diagnosed with laminitis. We felt this was stress induced, as one of our farriers had trimmed her feet back quite a lot and she was clearly uncomfortable. She was immediately stabled, with access to the yard during the day and her diet changed. I had been warned about this, but to find her barely able to stand or walk was very alarming.

She continued to be stabled for some time, until Micala decided she could be let out back into her paddock for a few hours each day, with her mates Victor, Herbie and Holly. My relationship with Peaches had not been as good as it was with some of the other horses up there. She was not often approachable and when being led in, could play up, as in rear up and kick out. However, being stabled seemed to mellow her and I was able to groom her and pick her feet out.

I knew she was getting better when she tried to bite me a few weeks ago. She has now fully recovered and is permanently out with her mates.

BELLA: RESCUED FROM THE MOOR WHEN SHE WAS A TINY FOAL.

Bonnie Bella, as I used to call her, is a small dark chestnut Welsh mare and was originally found on Dartmoor in the winter of 1978, when she was a tiny foal. A family were out walking on the moors when they came across her, shivering in the cold and nudging her dead mother. They were unsure what to do, but this plucky little foal followed them home and they kept her for several years. Eventually, when they were no longer able to look after her, they contacted Sylvia, the owner of the sanctuary at that time, who agreed to collect her.

Little is known about the period in Bella's life while she was first in Sylvia's care. Sylvia must have found a loan home for Bonnie at some stage, because I am told Bonnie was returned to our sanctuary much later on in her life in 2002, when she must have been around twenty four. She came with another horse called Cilla.

The girls at the sanctuary immediately set about getting the horses' feet shaved back and worked on getting them back into good condition, with a careful diet and lots of love and attention. Sometime later, people came to see Cilla and she went out on loan to them. She was given a 'forever home', as she was with them when she died, having spent her last years being loved and cared for.

Bonnie was also lucky. She was put out on loan to a lovely lady called Lucy who lives in Totnes. Lucy wanted another horse to keep her own horse company and she spoilt Bonnie. She was rugged and stabled every night. Unfortunately, Bonnie's luck ran out when Lucy's other horse had to be put to sleep and Lucy no longer needed another horse, so Bonnie was returned to us in 2014, aged thirty six.

She was put in with the 'oldies' at the time, Robin and Jess. For some reason, Sian changed her name from Bonnie to Bella, but I call her Bonnie Bella, so she had a connection to her old name. I never understand why people have to change the name of a horse when they get them. Surely, it is bad enough being uprooted from your home, without your new owner calling you by a name you don't recognise?

There is little mention of Bonnie-Bella in our earlier diaries, so I can only assume she was of good health. However, in May 2014 it is recorded that she had started to lose weight and by the end of the month her eating was so spasmodic, Kevin, our vet was called out. Sian suspected teeth trouble, but the vet also found a lump on one of her front legs and a cracked hoof.

Kevin removed one tooth and rasped back her other teeth as best as he could. However he said to complete the job, he required electricity for the rasping tool and we do not have any at the sanctuary. He was unable to complete the job how he would have liked. He also took a blood sample. Within a few days, our diary states that Bella "has eaten all her breakfast." Her blood test results were back on the 6th June. These showed she had liver disease, so the vet advised us to add a supplement to her feed. He also gave her a multi-vitamin injection that day.

Since 2014, thankfully, Bella's life had been without incident, until early in 2017 she lost her two companions Jess and Robin. We moved Pippin in with Bella, so she would not be on her own.

On our arrival one February, we found Bella with the chest strap from her rug stuck in her mouth! Goodness knows how she managed to do this, did we have another Jess on our hands? Jess regularly seemed to get into a mess with her rug. Bella's gums were bleeding, but she still managed to eat her breakfast.

Bella stabled early in 2017 for her feed.
Her rug was off as she had a good groom.

In March 2017, Angie and I notice that Bella's right eye was closed, so we bathed it with warm boiled water. I rang Julie who said she would bring up some warm tea the next day. I left a note in the diary for Sian to ask her to check the eye and she wrote in the diary the next day that 'Bella's eye was open and clean. Small patch of clouding on eye itself.'

A few days later Sian records that although Bella's eye was open, it was weeping. There was no indication whether the eye had been bathed or not. By this time, I was becoming concerned this might be an abscess and she might be in pain, so I spoke to Roland to see if he agreed to us calling our vet out. He did and in the meantime, Julie bought some drops for Bella's eye and started putting these in. These did not make any difference, so Sian was asked to get some from the Mole Valley vets.

When the vet arrived, he said poor Bella had an ulcer. He put drops in her eye and left these for us to apply one drop daily along her bottom lid. For the record, the vet said putting cold tea on bad eyes does not do any good.

Bella was in the wars again early in April and the vet was called out again. She was diagnosed with suspected colic and the vet also noticed that Bella's front legs appeared very stiff.

At that time, we had two more staff up at the sanctuary, so Bella almost had round the clock surveillance. Julie often came up to check on Bella later on in the day. On the advice of our vet, the regularity of her feeds were stepped up, so she was eating little and often. By the end of April, Kelly and I agreed we couldn't stand Bella being miserable and on her own for another day. She clearly missed Jess and Robin, so we moved Fie in with her as we felt it would solve two problems. Fie would be company for Bella and as Fie was getting bullied by the other four horses in her paddock at feed times, this would ensure that Fie was able to eat her feeds in peace.

Bella was so pleased to have some company, she went straight over to Fie, who promptly turned her back on her, flattened her ears and kicked Bella. The noise of the contact made us wince and we were horrified to see Bella limp away and favour the leg Fie had just kicked. Roland had always told me that if I were in any doubt, it was better to call a vet and he would be fine with that. So, I immediately rang ours and luckily, he was able to come over straight away.

It was with great relief that he told us nothing was broken. He prescribed a sachet of Danilon for Bonnie-Bella twice daily for a few days and then one a day for the next week. To our amazement, when we returned Bella to the paddock after the vet had gone, suddenly, Fie wanted her for her best mate. From that moment on, they were inseparable.

Unfortunately for Bella, within a few weeks, it became necessary to move Fie back in with her mates as she suddenly refused to eat. At that time, we were all scratching our heads to try and solve the problem of where to put which horses. Fie wouldn't eat when she was in with Bella and appeared to miss the Dartmoor's, Shannon and Bramble. However, when she was moved back in with them, she seemed indifferent to their presence. As she was being fed and they weren't, it meant she had to be caught twice daily to have her feed in the yard. This process always stressed her. There followed a period of swapping her back and forth, until she finally settled in with Bella when her mates were moved into the next paddock where she could see them.

Just when we thought things had settled down, Bella started eating irregularly during August and September, but Sian changed her food and she began to finish all her meals again.

During this time, I raised the question with the other girls, of whether we should get the dentist in for Bonnie-Bella. Her irregular eating had been addressed by changing her food, but I was certain her teeth were bad again. The last time she saw the dentist had been some years ago and I felt it was about time we got someone in to look at her teeth. In her present condition, she could not afford to lose weight, especially with winter coming up.

When Roland and Alison came over from France the following week, to pay a visit to the sanctuary and to meet up with us, I suggested we all met for lunch locally. I broached the subject when we were all together and he immediately agreed that with her history of bad teeth, we should get a dentist in. Luckily, Micala knew just the person. She booked him and within a few days, Keith arrived to look at both Bella and Fie.

Keith was not surprised Bella couldn't eat. She had four wobbly teeth, three of which he easily extracted immediately. There were no ligaments or nerves attached to these teeth anymore and decay had set in at the roots. The teeth would have been moving around in the soft tissue of her gums, causing discomfort and potentially, could have caused an infection risk. Had the teeth been left in, the abrasions the roots were causing could have led to abscesses and made eating very difficult and uncomfortable.

Bella barely batted an eye lid as these teeth practically fell out. Keith advised that the mouth would heal very quickly, from the bottom of the root upwards. This was a natural occurrence so the healing didn't trap any dirt in the wound.

He also rasped some of her sharp teeth down, to stop them cutting into her cheeks and tongue. In addition to the dental work, Keith advised putting Bella on a veteran diet which would help weight gain and would also improve her general condition. In his opinion, Bella was not ready to leave us yet and he felt that with a few diet tweaks, we would be able to get her back to tip top condition.

Unfortunately, Bella stopped eating again a few weeks after the dentist's visit. Micala changed her food again, but to no avail.

We all felt Bella's physical and mental condition was the result of being on her own now. Fie had been moved back in with her mates again a while ago, as she had stopped eating and was behaving erratically. Whilst none of us were happy that poor Bella was on her own again, we also knew that if she was put in with Fie and the other horses, they would eat her second feed, so she would still go hungry. Someone always needed to stand over her when she was eating if she was in with other horses, as it took her so long to eat her food these days.

We had a catch-22 situation, move Bella in with her mates which might stop her being depressed, or leave her on her own, so she could eat all of the two feeds a day we were giving her.

Roland was consulted and on the basis of the information Micala gave him regarding her failing physical and mental health; it was agreed that the vet would be called out. If he was of the opinion it was time for Bella to go, then she would be put to sleep during his visit.

The vet's visit fell on a Wednesday, which was my day up there. Angie, who had previously said she didn't want to be up there when any horse was put to sleep, kindly relented and came up with me for moral support. I was also relieved that Micala came up as well.

The time between us arriving at the sanctuary and the vet's arrival is interminable. The feeling of dread deepens as time ticks by. Angie took Bella's rug off and gave her a long groom whilst I did the rest of the chores.

It was a sunny day and watching Bella trot round her paddock in the sun, sticking her head over the fences to see her mates was heart wrenching. We began to wonder if we had made the wrong decision, but she hadn't eaten any of her breakfast and then we saw that she was very wobbly on her legs when she stood still. She seemed disoriented and was following us around, pushing into us for cuddles.

By the time the vet arrived Micala, Angie and I were on an emotional see-saw, still wondering if we were doing the right thing. However, our vet took one look at her and said it was time. Forty years was about to come to an abrupt end.

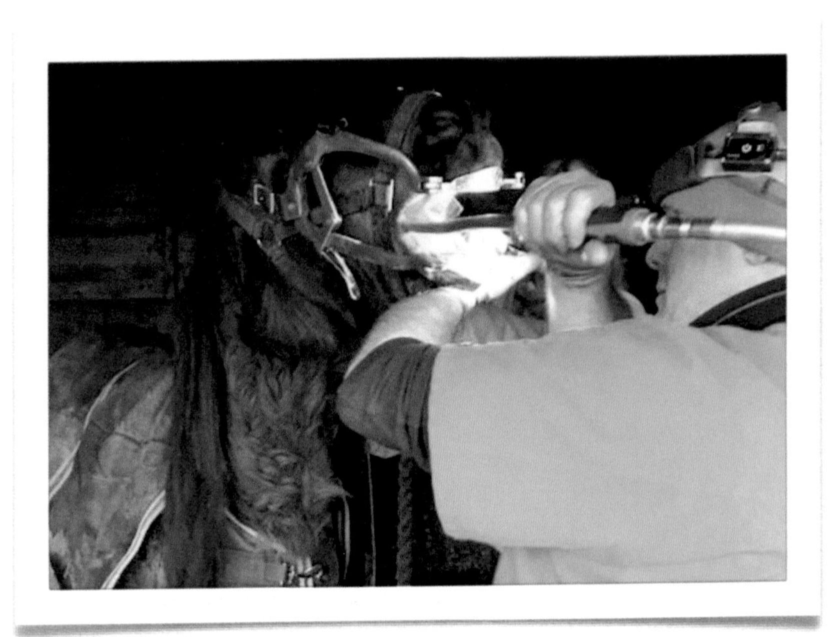

Bella gets her teeth sorted.

FAREWELL BELLA

Reflected in her lifeless eyes, were the silhouettes of our guilt.

In the gloom of the quiet stable,
we watched as the horse we loved slipped away,
Blue fluid coursing through her veins.

In the gloom of the quiet stable, we faced the result
of our reasoning and decision,
As the warmth of life ebbed away from her dead body.

Weighing heavily on us,
were the memories of her minutes before.
Trotting round her paddock, sun on her back,
peering over the fence at her mates
And following us, eager for cuddles.

We knew that in truth, Bella's forty years
had suddenly caught up with her.
Our doubts which had crept in, as our tears spilled out;
were surely un-founded.

In the gloom of the quiet stable, we knew we had released her
from her disinterest in eating
And her old body, which was failing.

I wished I could see her now.
Joining her past friends at Rainbow Bridge.
I imagined grazing heads would raise,
sensing an old friend had just arrived.
Greeting whinny's followed by the thundering of hooves,
as those friends galloped to meet her.
The sheer joy of their reunion, eclipsing the sorrow
of those of us left behind

....in the gloom of the quiet stable.

Safe journey Bella.

19/4/2018

BRAMBLE, SHANNON, BUSTER AND OUR DONKEY MIRANDA.

Bramble was already at the sanctuary when I started in 2011, but it is not clear exactly when he first arrived, although the girls had noted in our diary that he looked very skinny. They made sure he was fed regularly, but one morning in early April a few days after his arrival, they found him shivering, so they rugged him up and gave him extra food to warm him up.

A few weeks later he was in trouble with a swollen eye and our vet was called out. Within a few days, the eye was better and he was more his old self; in fact Sian recorded in our diary that he was looking very well and had gained weight. He was in trouble again a few days later with a deep cut on his chest and the girls decided that the barbed wire was the culprit. Although he made a full recovery from that incident, he became a solitary horse and spent a lot of time on his own and began pacing at the gate.

Some years later, in Mid-May, Roland was contacted by some people who expressed an interest in coming up to see Bramble, with a view to taking him out on loan. Prior to their visit, Sian took Bramble out for a ride, to see how he behaved outside the sanctuary. She found he rode well during the twenty minutes she was out with him and she had no problems with him, apart from the fact he refused to go anywhere near the farm which is just down the road from the sanctuary.

Sian rode Bramble out again late May and early June with Micala on another sanctuary horse, called Cider. Bramble was moved from his paddock during June to be with Lewis, as he was chasing a few of our other horses and distressing them. Bramble went out on loan to his new home in mid-June.

Following a home check by Sian early in February 2016, Bramble was returned to sanctuary at the end of that month. I was sad to learn his new home hadn't worked out, but excited to see him, as he had been at the sanctuary when I first started and I had fond memories of him. If you look on the DHAPS web site, you will see a picture of me with him when I first started, although the caption does say it is Fie!

On his return, Bramble was put in with Fie, Shannon and the Dartmoor's, Rudolph and Snowflake. I was worried to see he looked very skinny and his coat looked in very poor condition, but he seemed in good spirits. They say horses have good memories, so hopefully he remembered me when I ran over to him and gave him a massive cuddle.

Fie was instantly very smitten with Bramble and followed him around during his first day. I was quite piqued that she ignored me, but happy that he had a new companion. Nine months later, some people came up to see Bramble a few times and appeared keen to take him out on loan. However, although they promised to come up a third time at the end of November, sadly, they didn't turn up or even let us know they weren't coming. We never heard from them again.

Bramble is quite pushy at feed times and because he is really big, he can be quite daunting. Surprisingly, though, he is a very slow, gentle eater. Just after winter, when the grass was starting to struggle through, early in 2017, he showed how intelligent he is. He was still in with Fie, Shannon and the Dartmoor's and their large paddock had been halved with electrified tape, to allow the grass in the other half to grow. The area of paddock they were in was trampled and muddy and the little grass that came up was eaten immediately, so we planned to let them into the other side of the paddock, as soon as there was enough grass.

One morning, when Angie and I were pushing our wheel barrow over to his paddock, with feed and hay nets, I noticed that Bramble was on the other side of the electric tape, in the other paddock. However, the electric tape was still up and it didn't look as if it had been disturbed. Bramble was happily munching on the new grass there, but we were very puzzled as to how he had got in there.

Had he jumped over the electric wire? That was a plausible explanation, because he was a big horse and could have cleared it easily with a good run up. Whilst Angie set about feeding the others, I switched off the juice, took a section of the tape down and set about enticing Bramble back in with the others. He was not too keen to come back over even with a food bribe and it took a while to get him back in.

I had a rare light bulb moment and realised the only other

way he might have got into the other paddock was from behind the shelter. I knew this small gap had been fenced, but I walked over to check this and found that he too must have worked out that this was his only way in. He had then literally barged the small barricade down, stepped over it and smugly had the paddock to himself. None of the other horses had followed him.

I had new respect for him after that, although it took me about an hour to put the barricade back up behind the shelter. For good measure, I also ran some rope from the other back corner of the shelter into the hedge, to put him off getting through my new defences. He was no longer the horse that became intimidating at feed times, he was the brains of the sanctuary.

Angie grooming Bramble, April 2017

In March of 2017, Bramble had more visitors. However, nothing ever came of that either and in October that year, Roland decided that Bramble should go over to France with Shannon and Buster.

The plan was that all three horses were to go over to France before the end of the year, while the ferries were still running. Shannon and Bramble would stay with Roland's friends for the winter, but would return to Brantome the following summer. Roland wanted Buster over in France to be trained at their sanctuary at Brantome, to work with handicapped children, a new venture set up by Roland and Alison earlier on in 2017. He felt Buster's gentle nature would be very well suited to the work he had in mind.

Buster had arrived with us at the sanctuary in June 2016. He was a quarter horse, crossed with a Connemara. He had a cream coat and dark brown mane and his owner described his character as cheeky but strong. Unfortunately, she was no longer able to keep him, as she was moving house and where she was going had no paddocks in the immediate vicinity. Buster arrived with very little of his tail, as one of the companions he had been in a field with had eaten most of it. He was put in a paddock with Snoopy and Pippin.

He had a lovely nature and settled in with us very quickly. He was easy to handle and was a very inquisitive horse. His short time with us, before he went over to France, was uneventful. In preparation for his move, we started to bring him in to the stable and groom him daily. He responded very well to this new regime.

Buster was Angie's first foray into handling our larger horses. I had been encouraging her to groom the smaller ones and practice putting head collars on them, as that was how I had learnt. Buster had such a lovely nature, Angie was very comfortable putting a head collar on him and leading him in for his feed. She was soon grooming him and this helped her confidence enormously.

By the end of October, on Roland's instructions, Sian was taking Buster out of the sanctuary for walks around the lanes. She then started to ride him around the paddocks of the sanctuary. It had been a few years since he had been ridden by his previous owner but he slipped back into the regime like it had been yesterday. Sian started to 'hack out' Buster in early November and was very pleased with how he behaved.

Whilst I was delighted that these horses would be in a better climate and have more attention, I was quite upset to be losing both Bramble and Shannon. I had formed quite an emotional attachment to both of them. I was also worried about how Fie was going to react, losing her best mate Shannon.

Unfortunately, I cannot write much about Shannon, as little is known about her. Over the years since I started work at the sanctuary, her life has, mostly been free of injury and drama. She has been stabled a few times with abscesses in her hooves. One March, the vet stated after examining her that she had "the worst abscess he had ever seen".

She was not happy at having the hoof in question picked out, so he had to sedate her, to enable him to clean her hoof out and put a poultice on. He said she should be stabled for five days and put on Bute and the poultice should be changed daily. He said her hoof should be immersed in a bucket of tolerably hot water with Epson salts in, then a new poultice put on. Roland said let her out into the paddock and keep an eye on her, so that is what we did!

So, prior to her journey to France, during October, a visit from our vet was arranged to check Shannon was chipped and to check and if necessary update her passport. Sian had contacted me the day before, to ask me to put a head collar on Shannon when I arrived the next day, as the vet was coming at 11 am.

I made (the wrong) assumption that as Shannon was not in the yard when I got there, that Sian had confirmed with the vet that we would walk down to Shannon's paddock. What I should have done, was go and get Shannon in, because when she arrived, the vet was not too happy having to trudge down across two very large and muddy paddocks to inspect her.

Shannon was, as always, very approachable and easy to catch. Unfortunately, her companions, the two Dartmoor's and Bramble wanted in on the action. It proved impossible to bring Shannon in on her own to the adjoining paddock, as the other three barged through the gate before the vet could shut it. The vet had to examine Shannon, check her chip and take details down about her markings for her passport with three other horses milling around, poking their noses into her pockets and in her notes, to see what she was up to.

By late November all three passports were ready and the transporter had been booked for the three of them to go to France on either the 15th or 16th of December, depending on the weather for the ferry and on the transportation company's schedule.

On Wednesday 13th December, Kelly came up to help move Bramble and Shannon from their paddocks, up to the stables, in preparation for their transportation to France. We were not sure the exact date the transporter would be arriving and it was agreed it was best to be prepared for the earlier date. I maned the gates and as Kelly wanted more experience of leading big horses, she led Bramble up first, then Shannon. They were no trouble at all, but puzzled and nervous at being stabled.

Kelly bribes Shannon with carrots,
prior to putting her new head collar on.

Friday 15th December dawned and Kelly woke with a feeling of dread. This was the day the transporter would arrive at Manaton and she would be on her own to work with the transporter staff and walk down to the village with Buster, Shannon and Bramble.

Neither I nor Sian could be there to help. Sian at least had a good excuse, she had a hospital appointment. But me? Well, I could have been there if I am honest, but I bottled out due to the sheer emotional drain of it all, having done this many times before. Roland had assured both Kelly and I that there would be at least two men from the transporter company to help, who were used to doing this; so I didn't feel too bad. Poor Kelly was really stressed about it so her fiancé Martin came up to the sanctuary in the morning. He stayed as late as he could, but had to leave before the transporter got there, as he was doing the school run for their children.

I don't think Kelly was stressed because she had to lead the horses. I think it was the emotional part of the process she found stressful. Saying goodbye to horses you have come to love is horrible. I said my teary goodbyes to them on the Wednesday we moved them.

Kelly's very modest diary entry for her heroic deeds that day were: "Walked the three horses down to the lorry." She kindly rang me after the transporter had left to take our horses to their future life in France. We were both in tears, a mixture of relief all went well and because we would miss all three of them.

Buster's training at the Brantome sanctuary in France is still ongoing. Roland's granddaughter Chloe is spending a lot of time with him, so he has regular contact with children. In addition to helping children with disabilities, Buster is also helping elderly people with learning difficulties. Each week, these people groom and feed Buster and it has added a joy and purpose to their lives. Later in 2018, Roland had arranged for a group of people from a residential home for adults with severe disabilities to go up to the sanctuary at Brantome, to groom Buster.

Both Shannon and Bramble are thriving and happy in their new home with Roland's friends.

Miranda was a grey female donkey who was bought by a family when she was eight months old, to grow up with their children. She had been a loved family pet since then and she was very well looked after and had a wonderful life. Unfortunately, when the parent's marriage failed and they split up, she was no longer wanted, particularly because by this time the children had grown up and left home. An all too common a story for poor horses and donkeys these days.

Sylvia was asked if she could take Miranda in and offer her a 'forever home', which she quite happily did. Miranda arrived at the Hillside sanctuary in April 2000 to keep another grey donkey, Sammy, company, but she was moved to the Southcott site in September 2011, when Sammy died of cancer. The sanctuary at Southcott only has two close neighbours, a farm and a private cottage. These people were to get to know the very loud 'EEAW' which Miranda used to greet us and any visitors. Sometimes she would quite happily continue this racket for hours at a time.

At Southcott, Miranda became the constant companion of a little grey pony but after a few years this little pony also died and from then on she never really seemed to find anyone else to pair up with, but luckily, seemed happy in her own company. As we did not want her to be lonely, she was placed in a paddock near the yard, so she had the company of the horses in the next paddock and us when we were up there working. When anyone arrived at the sanctuary, she would come running up 'EE AWING' very loudly. Never has anyone had such a fantastic greeting! When I first started at the sanctuary, hers was the best welcome I ever got and to this day, no horse has ever beaten that.

Despite her angelic appearance, Miranda, like the horses, was very pushy when it came to feeding time. She was known to bite if she thought you were taking too long to give her food bowl to her. When she was let out into the yard, she quickly found out where the food was kept in the barn and learnt that if she knocked the lids off the bins, she could get a good feed.

Shortly after I arrived at the sanctuary, Miranda went through a tough time when she was scratching a lot, so our vet was contacted and he gave her a spray and some shampoo which would calm the irritation down. However, this did not seem to work, so the girls resorted to spraying her with tee-tree oil and used a purple antiseptic spray on her. Our diary at that times states: "Miranda is not impressed with the vet shampoo, but it may have helped her dandruff."

Some days she was very subdued and was found lying down, although she got up fast enough when she heard the feeds being prepared. She was always rugged in the winter when the weather was very cold. Her health, towards the end of her life, became un-predictable. She developed a habit of chewing her food and spitting it out. As she grew older, her eyes became very weepy, so the girls regularly put tea bags on Miranda's eyes to sooth them and they groomed her regularly. They also walked her to Manaton Green and back, when they had time.

Miranda was thirty-five when she died, on the 3rd of May 2012. The vet was called out to her but by the time he arrived, she had sadly passed. Diary entries for this week are sparse, but I believe Miranda got marooned on a large muck heap in her paddock. She somehow got through the tape which had been put up to stop her doing just that, and fell down one side of it. We think her struggle to get up caused her death.

This was my first experience of losing an animal at the sanctuary and it hit me hard.

Her old family were informed. They wanted to have a blessing to celebrate her life and true to their word, they arrived at the sanctuary on a very rainy day. Both Debbie and Alison were there to meet them and the service was conducted by the son. It was a very poignant affair and we were so pleased that Miranda's life could be remembered like this. We all remarked on how quiet it now was at Southcott, without Miranda braying all the time. I am sure the neighbours were hugely relieved though.

Following her death, I planted a shrub in my garden in her memory and it blooms every year. It makes me smile when I look at it and remember her loud welcomes and lively personality - it is good to remember those that have passed on from the sanctuary.

STAFF AND VOLUNTEERS AT SOUTHCOTT: THE LIFE BLOOD OF THE SANCUTARY. 2010 - 2018

Roland's introduction to this book makes it clear that without the dedication and support of the full time members of staff and volunteers, the Devon Horse and Pony Sanctuary would not be where it is today. I thought therefore, it is only right to include a bit about these people, as some of them are only mentioned fleetingly elsewhere in this book.

It annoys me when I buy books about rescue animals and find what I think is far too much detail about the people side of things. So, I have put this chapter at the end of the book, so you can skip it if you want. I have also tried to keep this information to a minimum, as I think if you have bought this book, you did so because you wanted to read the stories of our rescued horses, not all about me and the staff. However, as Roland quite rightly pointed out, we make the sanctuary in Devon tick.

You will know from reading 'How it all began: Sylvia sets up the sanctuary: Lucky's Legacy', that the owners of our Sanctuary on Dartmoor now live in the Dordogne, France. They set up and run the 'Brantome Police Horses and Friends' sanctuary for retired English Police horses. I think it is important to show that although they live in France, they work hard to support whoever is currently managing the sanctuary.

Although Roland and Alison are frequent visitors to our sanctuary in Devon, they have entrusted the responsibilities of the day to day running of our Devon Sanctuary to various people over the years. When I first started at the sanctuary in 2011, there were three girls working up there; Sian, Leanne and Micala. At that time, the sanctuary was managed by Debbie, Roland and Alison's daughter. When Debbie and her family moved over to France to live with her parents and set up a wedding business, Roland relied on his staff in Devon to run the sanctuary.

Sian had joined Leanne and Micala a year prior to my arrival, when she responded to an advert in the local paper.

Micala had originally started work at our sanctuary in 2010, a year before I started. She was working locally at a Field Study

Centre, Colehay's Park and heard another member of staff talking about how fed up she was with her other job. Micala asked her where that job was and it turned out it was at our Devon Horse and Pony Sanctuary.

Micala had lots of experience working with horses, as she had previously worked at local racing stables. She was keen to work with horses again, so she asked this girl if she thought she might be able to take her place at the sanctuary. Following a chat with Roland, she was able to replace the girl who left. Initially, Micala worked at the Hillside Stables part of the sanctuary, where ten of the sanctuary horses were. Her job included mucking out ten stables, feeding and making sure they all had fresh water.

The three girls each had allotted days when they worked and they divided their time between both the Southcott and Hillside sanctuaries. The amount of time spent at each site depended on how many horses there were at each one, at any given time.

Back when Sian first started, the basic work at the two sanctuaries was much the same as it is today. This included feeding, poo picking the paddocks and shelters, mucking out stables and making sure there was fresh water in all the paddocks and occupied stables. The girls also handled the horses as much as possible, ensuring feet were picked out, the horses were groomed regularly and where time allowed, they used to walk some of the horses out in the lanes around the sanctuaries.

Often, horses would be ridden from Hillside to Southcott if they needed to be moved. If there was time after all the chores had been done, the girls would also ride out some of the horses at the sanctuary, Bramble and Cider were their favourites. This was good for the horses, as it broke up the boredom for them.

In the early days, communication between the girls was via the site diaries. I am not sure this was a very good form of communication, because one would write 'we need more food' or 'someone needs to go to Mole Valley for Citronella Cream' and no one would end up doing it because one of them would think the others would be buying the necessary items. However, things got done in the end by someone and the situation improved when one of them was appointed Manager.

The diaries were also used to record what had been done each day and any concerns either of them had on one of the horses.

They were used to admonish as well. Particularly me. You will have read in the book how messages were left for me, in capitals and underlined when I did something wrong in my early months. To be fair, this stopped after I asked the girls to ring me if they found I had done something wrong, so we could discuss how I could do better.

Leanne and Micala left the sanctuary about a year after I arrived, in 2012, due to growing families and other commitments. Over the next two years, this left Sian to do six days a week and me the Wednesdays and holiday cover when needed. About two years after I had been going up there on my own, a friend at the time, Karen, said she wanted to 'Come up to see what you do every Wednesday and help out'.

I was thrilled to show her the sanctuary and the horses, but at the same time, I was concerned whether she would enjoy working up there, because she wasn't the kind of person I envisaged doing that sort of work. She wasn't what I would call the 'out-doors' type. I struggled to see how someone who led a fairly sedentary lifestyle would take to the heavy work we had to do up there, such as poo picking and wheeling a barrow laden with food and hay nets across large paddocks in all weathers. In addition, she had no experience with horses, no affinity with them and was honest enough to say she would be very nervous around them.

I was really pleased when, having spent a day at the sanctuary with me helping with the chores, she said she wanted to come up with me each Wednesday and become a member of our team. During the next three years, even if she was feeling un-well, she came up with me every Wednesday. She did a great job and was not fazed by the weather, or the physically demanding chores.

She went out and bought boots and waterproofs, she helped when Cider needed his treatment and learnt how to put head collars on, lead horses, groom and rug them. Shannon was her favourite horse and over the years Karen bought her new winter rugs and each week turned up with large bags of chopped carrots. We tried to do a bit of DIY when fencing was down, cross rails were broken and shelters needed repairing. We called ourselves 'Bodge-it-and-Scarper'.

She even offered to share the driving, which was great, as it reduced my petrol expenses. Not only did she work hard up there, but she provided great moral support for me when the horses fell ill and particularly when we lost several of them early in 2014. Somehow, between getting drenched and cold in the winter and bitten by horse flies in the summer, we managed to have a good laugh.

Karen even used to go up to the sanctuary on her own when I was away on holiday. I thought that was very brave of her, especially as her first shift didn't start well, when cows blocked the road on the moor on the way up to the village of Manaton. She didn't want to get out of the car, but waited until a local came along, stopped and shoed them out of the way. During her time with us, she was kicked by Vera when leading her out of her paddock up to the stables, but this incident didn't put her off either. Over the years, she came to know and love all the horses but she was forced to stop coming up due to ill health.

More regular help was to come in 2014. You will have read in Cider's chapter that Julie and Bryan responded to Sian's desperate call for help when Cider had his accident, getting tangled in the barbed wire. Following that terrible incident, they started to come up to the sanctuary regularly, initially to give Sian moral support during that terrible time at the beginning of 2014 when we lost so many horses in quick succession.

When things settled down at the sanctuary, Julie decided she would still like to carry on helping there. She asked if she could become an official volunteer so she could continue to help Sian out with the feeding and poo picking. Julie's husband Bryan had already noticed the place was crying out for a lot of maintenance work; including repairing shelters and fencing. He too decided this would be an ideal project for him a few days a week, so they both became volunteers.

We don't have electricity at Southcott, as we are in a very remote location, so the cost would be prohibitive. When I first started working at the sanctuary, I bought a camping gas stove and some gas canisters, so we were able to make ourselves hot drinks in the winter. In addition, the hot water came in handy when any of the horses needed wounds bathed. One of the first things Bryan did was to get hold of an old portable generator, which Roland paid for. We were able to use an 'electric kettle', which didn't take ages to boil, to make cups of tea and coffee. The generator is also used for charging up power tools and to provide light in the gloom of the barn during winter.

Following the repair and installation of our little generator, Bryan decided his next project was to build us a shelter to house our massive round bales of hay. Historically, due to there being nowhere else to put them, bales of hay were kept outside, either in the yard, or the top paddock. However, in bad weather, it was like a scene from 'Far From the Madding Crowd' when we would be trying to throw large horse rugs over the huge bales in driving rain and high winds, trying to secure them, to keep the rain off the hay. Invariably, the next day, the hay would be soaked through as the horse blankets would have been torn off. Someone then had the bright idea of storing the hay bales in our fourth stable. However, we were unable to use this, because during our run of ill horses, early in 2014, all stables were occupied.

The new hay store was made of wood and Bryan made the floor from disused railway sleepers. Roland paid for the sleepers, but Julie and Bryan paid for the wood. Shortly after the completion of the hay shelter, someone reported us to the Dartmoor National Parks. Their rules state that any permanent building needs their permission. Fortunately, as it is made of wood and does not have a concrete floor, it is not deemed to be a permanent structure, so the inspector who came out allowed us to keep it, thank goodness.

Bryan was on a roll now and turned his attention to our really old and rusting green tractor. It looked to me like it should be in a museum. I was certain no amount of coaxing would encourage it to come to life or ever be used again – apart from by Luna, our rescued yard cat, who used to curl up on the old seat and go to sleep on it in the summer. However, Bryan persuaded a friend to come up and have a look at it. Following the installation of lots of new parts, which Roland also paid for and a lot of TLC, this chap got it going again. It turned out it was worth the hard work, as it proved to be invaluable when we had to put up new fencing.

Julie organised a 'fencing day', which involved about thirteen of us working at the sanctuary one Saturday, taking down barbed wire and replacing this with post and rail fencing. Taking barbed wire down is an awful, time consuming job. The clips which had been used to secure it to the wooden posts had long rusted so they were impossible to pull out. We had to cut the wire either side of the posts and protecting our hands with heavy gloves, wind the stuff up and put it in a wheel barrow. In a lot of cases, because the posts had been in a very long time, they had rotted at the base and quite a lot came out during the process.

We also segregated some of our larger paddocks with this new fencing, to enable us to rest more paddocks, allowing the grass to recover. Simon, the man who mended our tractor, managed to beg/borrow a gadget from somewhere which attached to the tractor, so it could be used to put the posts in. There is no way we could have done this without the tractor, as there are so many boulders up there and the ground is very hard.

At the end of this long, very tiring day, one of our helpers cooked sausages and burgers on the BBQ. Sian had made cakes the night before and we used the gas burners to keep people in tea and coffee. Roland, as a gesture of thanks, paid for all the food. Our tractor is used regularly now, for chain harrowing (towing a chain with spikes on to break up the horse poo in the paddocks) and pulling a small trailer when needed.

For me, one of the best things Bryan did, was provide a supply of water to all the water containers in our paddocks. We had a few troughs and these were fed via water pipes, long ago dug deep into the fields. The large plastic water containers in the paddocks were filled courtesy of us lugging five gallon water containers to them in our wheel barrow each day. Sian, who was the right side of twenty-five and a keep fit fanatic, had relished this work because it was "toning up my arms". Those of us who are the wrong side of fifty were not so happy.

One day, Bryan looked up from his DIY and watched us struggling with these containers in the wheelbarrow and decided enough was enough. He asked if Roland would pay for some water pipes and new troughs for the paddocks where the containers were. Roland agreed, so Bryan installed and connected a network of blue water pipes to the new troughs.

When winter began approaching, we all started to nag our local farmer Brian, who had agreed to come in and dig out trenches to enable Bryan to bury the water pipes, so they didn't freeze when the weather grew icy. The work was done in plenty of time for the winter of 2015.

Our days of carrying large, very heavy five gallon containers to each of the paddocks, which was back breaking, painful work, were finally over. Painkillers would no longer be needed after that chore. Thanks to Roland's funding and Bryan's hard work, all paddocks now have self-filling troughs. All we have to do is clean them out regularly.

In my opinion, the second best thing Bryan did was to make a small wooden structure to house our chemical toilet. Fantastic, no more stripping down outside in the winter, in driving rain, high winds or snow for a wee! Paintings by Sian's daughter Lola hid the natural holes in the wood and postcards I have sent from foreign holidays also cheer the tiny room up.

Bryan put up partitions between the stables, so there would be no more fights if two horses who don't care for each other were in close proximity. He also purchased and put up strong rubber mats on the walls, to protect these against those of our herd who like to kick the walls and in the process make lots of noise which could annoy our nearest neighbour.

Using our ancient tractor, Bryan also moved a couple of field shelters. The first one to be moved was in one of our larger paddocks, which had two shelters. Before work could start to segregate this paddock with new fencing, one of the two shelters had to be moved over, so that both halves would have a shelter. A second shelter was moved to the top of a sloping paddock, so it wouldn't get flooded in the winter as the water poured into the yard and streamed down into it.

Bryan carried out all sorts of repair work, including repairing wooden gates which had suffered years of abuse by humans and horses alike. Catches were repaired, new gate posts dug in. Weeds throughout the sanctuary were strimmed and burnt. Both Julie and Bryan trimmed back the hedges behind all the field shelters, in preparation for these shelters being creosoted. Most of us chipped in with this work, which was not pleasant. This work could only be carried out in the summer, when the weather was dry. We looked like something out of the cast of 'Breaking Bad', with our white all in one protective suits, eye googles and masks. Angie and I did about three shelters in the very hot weather and our goggles kept steaming up. Neither of us like being up ladders, but we managed to get the work done.

Bryan appears to have the starring role in his and Julie's work at the sanctuary, but she has been at his side and helped during most of his DIY work, as well as helping with the day to day chores. Do not underestimate the amount of physical effort it takes every day to poo pick large paddocks, some with six horses in it.

In 2015 another friend of mine, Angie, came up, like Karen did, to "see what you do" and is, at the time of writing (2019) still helping on Wednesdays. She does have a bit more of a background with horses, as, like me, she spent time riding in her younger years, so she had less to learn than Karen.

A few years later, early in 2017, I approached Roland, to tell him I thought we still were a bit thin on the ground. We had only one paid person up there (Sian) and myself, Angie, Julie and Bryan volunteering. There had been occasions where Sian, Julie and Bryan had taken their holidays at the same time and it fell to me to provide cover for these weeks. Whilst I didn't mind, I felt this left us very vulnerable if I couldn't get up there for any reason who would feed and check our horses?

In addition, I had been concerned that for some time, that due to family and other work related commitments, Sian was struggling to spend quality time at the sanctuary. She was also desperate to spend some more time with her young daughter at weekends. Eventually, she told Roland she could no longer work at the sanctuary on those days. This meant Roland was relying solely on volunteers for working at the sanctuary Saturday and Sundays. Whist the loyalty and hard work we volunteers put in went without question, I felt we might be vulnerable to matters outside any of our control and we should take on at least two new paid staff.

Roland and Alison were aware of the situation and agreed with me. He asked me to word an advert for two paid members of staff. He and Alison came over in April 2017, to interview two people, who they thought would make good members of our team. He said they were happy to cover weekends and holidays. They would fill the gap Sian had left at weekends and we wouldn't have to worry about holiday cover as there would now be three paid members of staff and of course the four volunteers. Initially, we were all optimistic that this level of staffing would bring us not only flexibility, but a good depth of knowledge across all platforms of equine care.

I first met Lara on the 5th April, when Roland brought her up to the sanctuary, following her interview. It was pouring with rain, so the sanctuary certainly did not look at its best. Roland gave her a quick tour of the paddocks and Lara met all our horses. She certainly seemed to be very self-assured and knowledgeable about everything equine. The second successful candidate, Kelly, was due to start work at sanctuary for the first time the next day.

Kelly had a bit of a baptism of fire on her first day. Sian had found Pippin in pain when she arrived and had to call the vet out, as she suspected Pippin had Colic. Following the vets visit, Sian showed Kelly our daily routine. I first met Kelly when I came up to see Fie, on Saturday 8th April. She and Lara were on duty together that day. I took to Kelly immediately. Of the two, Lara was clearly the more confident one and perhaps the more knowledgeable about horses. However, Kelly was very eager and keen to learn more about the care of our horses.

Having new people at the sanctuary felt a bit weird. We were entrusting our beloved horses to people we didn't know. I worried they might not lock the place up when they left. Would they love the horses as we did? Would they get up there nice and early to feed them? Of course they would and they did.

In order for me to get to know Kelly and vice versa, Roland suggested she came up on a Wednesday, just for a few weeks, to work with Angie and I. I realised that this would present us with a good opportunity to standardise her training and help her to get to know us and feel like she was a part of our team. It would also help us by getting used to having new people up there and hopefully learning to trust them with our horses. Any worries I had about the new girls were very short lived. Both Lara and Kelly were lovely people and very keen to learn the ropes and interact with all our horses.

Whilst it was good having extra people with us, soon some of us felt we now had 'too many cooks', seven to be precise. Obviously not all of us were up there at the same time, but we all had our own methods and opinions as to how to do things and manage problems. Every year horses are rotated throughout our many paddocks and even this caused a bit of bad feelings, as some of us were not party to discussions as to which horses should be moved, when and where. Even though Angie was constantly reminding me that as a volunteer, maybe I didn't deserve a voice, I felt I had been up there long enough to be able to have a say in what went on. Turning up to do my shift to find out horses had been moved around and there was nothing in the diary to say why and where, used to wind me up and I was constantly reminding the others to keep the diary up to date.

One day Angie and I spent over thirty minutes looking for two horses we couldn't find during our checks. We hurried up to the barn to ring Sian, only to be told the two in question had gone out on loan the previous day!

There were constant debates about which horses should be fed, what type of food and in what quantities. This arose every year as winter approached and in 2017, the debate was made worse, because all of us wanted a say in what was to be done. When Lara and Kelly were appointed, Lara had lots to say about whether hay was given or not, even down to the point of wanting to change the type of hay nets we used. However, her suggestion to change the food Bella was having was very well received. New broom, new eyes, new ideas.

The cause of the problem was clear to me. We had seven people up there without any clear leadership from one person when decisions needed to be made. We needed someone to step up and become manager. I had told Roland I was happy to do this, but of course and quite rightly, he wanted a paid member of staff to take on this responsibility. I was only up there 1-2 days a week.

Roland had previously appointed Sian 'Yard Manager', but as she was increasingly spending less and less time at the sanctuary, Roland asked Lara to step up. For my money, Lara was the best choice, due to her personality and experience, but she was reluctant to do so, concerned about stepping on Sian's toes. This was a very frustrating time for me, as I was still very keen to manage the place but I wasn't given the opportunity. What made it worse for me, was the fact no one else wanted the responsibility.

Lara suggested to Roland that perhaps she could manage the horse side of things and I could be the 'yard manager'. I was already ordering and collecting the feeds, because during that time, we sometimes used to run out of food for the horses. This used to drive me up the wall as I frequently arrived at the sanctuary to find we had little feed left to feed all the horses, which resulted in me having to drive back down to Mole Valley and get food I could have collected on the way up.

I was also managing a 'maintenance schedule' of the DIY work Bryan did. I kept receipts and compiled spreadsheets of our monthly spend and I sent these to Roland so he could keep an eye on our expenditure and these also helped the charity's accountant. I also organised regular team meetings, as I felt now there were seven of us, it was important we met face to face regularly. These meetings allowed us to discuss plans to move horses around, feeding regimes and clear up any misunderstandings which had arisen by any poor communications. I also made sure, by liaising with our farmer neighbour Brian, that we never ran out of hay. I seemed to be the only person who had the knack of catching our busy farmer neighbour for the bales of hay he supplied.

Roland was adamant that Lara run everything, so he offered the Managers job to her, rejecting her idea of her just doing the horses and me managing the other side of it. He was right, of course, and very soon, Lara was running the place with confidence and ease.

Angie and I took some time out after our chores for several Wednesdays, sorting out old horse rugs, labelling the ones we decided to keep and taking the others to St Luke's Hospice in Plymouth, who turned them into blankets after cleaning. Angie kept the barn tidy and regularly burnt our rubbish. We also did some DIY when fences were down on our arrival. Bodget-and-scarper-V2!

Kelly's fiancé Martin started to come up and help us with running repairs and DIY. This was great, as we now had two people keeping the weeds down and chain harrowing the paddocks, as Bryan was still doing his bit.

Lara's first decision was to instigate a 'horse handling' regime.

She quite rightly pointed out that some of our horses were practically feral and needed a lot more handling. We had been happy to let them get on with their lives but the lack of handling had become an issue when the farrier was due.

Roland agreed that more handling had to be done, but this created a conflict for him. He had two additional people to pay and they were now, on his request, working together for safety reasons during handling. This meant they were spending more time up at the sanctuary after they had finished the chores. Wage bills were rising.

While Roland was worrying about wage bills, I was now happy with the way things were going and delighted that communications between all of us at the sanctuary had improved since Lara had officially taken up the reigns. Lara or Kelly would text or ring me before my shift Wednesday, if they had made any changes at the sanctuary, for example, moving horses around.

As the days Sian worked at the sanctuary gradually decreased and she asked for cover at weekends, it became obvious that Kelly and Lara may not have fully understood they were expected to work Saturday and Sundays. There had clearly been a misunderstanding during their interviews, when Roland said he had explained to them that he needed them to cover at weekends, as Sian wanted to spend more time with her daughter. Kelly and Lara also had young families and other commitments, so they were, understandably, not keen to work at weekends either.

When they had only been with us a few weeks, I had to cover a few weekends while Lara and Kelly worked out a weekend rota between them. Unfortunately, we were to face another big change, as Julie and Bryan left the sanctuary at the end of April, 2017, due to Bryan's ill health.

Another blow was to follow. Lara left us quite suddenly a short time later. Her last diary entry was 11th July. She said she wasn't happy when her hours were reduced, she had become too emotionally involved with our horses and finally, she also felt she was not able to spend enough time with her family at weekends.

I had learnt a lot from her. She taught me the best way to

approach and catch horses, the correct way to lead them, the right type of hay nets to buy, when to worm the horses and much more. Even with her other commitments, she very often worked longer up the sanctuary than she was paid to do. I was worried that things would go back to how they were before she arrived, not enough horse handling.

Lara left a legacy of many improvements. Our 'First Aid Box' was re-stocked. She had tidied and kept the yard clear of rubbish. She had worked on our most difficult horses, so they were much easier to handle.

My beloved Fie, our most un-predicable and sometimes unapproachable horse, was now caught daily and led in to the yard for her feeds. Under Lara's guidance, she had quickly learnt that lead rope equalled food and became very easy to catch. Very soon, Fie was also comfortable with being fed in a stable and she was having her feet picked out regularly, as well as being groomed by all, not just me.

Snoopy was also being brought in for his feed. Snoopy particularly needed regular handling as he was young and wilful. I at no point led Snoopy anywhere, I just opened the gate to the yard and he thundered in to a stable for his food. I am an alive cowardly-custard. Kelly took a shine to Buster and was working with him daily.

We were now down from seven people to four. Kelly, Sian, me and Angie. Kelly's confidence grew from day to day and she had a natural rapport with all the horses up there. Her fiancé Martin, took over all the maintenance and repairs at the sanctuary. Martin also taught me how to start and drive the tractor.

He had a busy year in 2017. He put up new metal gates, fenced off areas of paddocks previously having barbed wire. He fixed leaky troughs, put up new fence posts and electrified paddocks as they were put into use. He put new sections of roofing on leaking shelters and chain harrowed paddocks where necessary. Within a few months of him coming up, my worries about how the place would be maintained after Bryan left began to recede.

We continued to try our best to carry on Lara's legacy even when Kelly and Sian's hours were reduced in the approach to winter. The weather up on Dartmoor in the winter is not conducive to hanging around. Driving rain, slippery and deep mud, sleet, snow and freezing conditions make this a dangerous environment to handle some of our horses. On this basis, Roland decided that for their safety, Kelly and Sian should not risk handling and go back to working alone on separate days.

Sian had increased her hours during the week, to help us out when Lara left, but she was still adamant that she wouldn't work at weekends. I began to worry again about the lack of cover if anyone was away on holiday or needed a day off. When Kelly was away for two weeks at the end of July, Sian pitched in, so I only had to cover one weekend and one Monday.

However, all was not well. By September 2017, Sian's diary entries regarding horse handling, feeding and other chores became sparse. At times, she only wrote one line in the diary, which made it difficult for the rest of us to understand whether horses had received their feeds and supplements.

When Sian went away for two weeks in September, Kelly did the lion's share of the cover, with me doing one day at the weekend to give her a break, to spend time with her family. Kelly was now very confident around the horses. She was moving horses around as she saw fit and was making decisions she wouldn't have felt confident to make and implement a few months previously.

Late September, Sian asked Roland if it would be ok if she asked Micala to come back to the sanctuary, just to cover for the odd day at the weekends. Kelly needed more time off with her family. Micala returned to work at the sanctuary on Sunday 8th October 2018.

Micala is used to working with massive, skittish race horses, so she was not fazed by the behaviour of some of our more nervous ones. She is very committed to our horses and takes great care of them. She now has head collars on those who we haven't been able to catch since Lara left and is very knowledgeable on all aspects of horse management and care.

Early December 2017, I wrote in the diary that once again, we were very low on food, the feed bins were nearly empty. I asked Kelly if she could do a bulk order at Mole Valley, to see us through Christmas and New Year. Sian had indicated she would not want to work another Christmas, which was fair enough, as she had worked pretty much all of them up to now. As luck would have it, Roland and Alison were over from France and volunteered for these shifts. The food was bulk ordered and delivered in plenty of time, which was good because the weather was really cold with forecasts of a white Christmas up on the moor.

It did indeed snow on the 9th, 10th and 11th December. Feeds and hay were increased. By Thursday 21st December we were ready for Christmas. Food bins were all stocked up and I wrote up Roland's guidance for the feeding regime on our white board in the barn. Christmas cards were written and left by the four of us girls for each other. During the worst of the snow, Micala was the only person who made it up to the sanctuary, through the deep drifts to feed our horses.

All seemed well. However, on the 21st, Roland and Sian had a disagreement and that day was to be her last ever at the sanctuary.

Roland wrote in our diary on 22nd December: 'New regime starts today. Kelly now in charge.' He had asked Brian the farmer to deliver massive round bales of hay to each shelter in use and we were to ensure this never ran out. This was to enable the horses to have unlimited access to hay in the bad weather and also meant we didn't have to spend time filling up loads of hay nets. Another added benefit of this new regime was that if the snow got so deep and no one could get up there, at least the horses had loads of hay in their shelters.

The other, much welcome change, was that we were no longer to poo pick the bigger paddocks, only the shelters. He asked Martin to continue to chain harrow these paddocks when weather permitted. That was great news for all of us, who were getting exhausted battling wheel barrows full of poo up through muddy or the deep ruts in the frozen paddocks.

During his Christmas shift, Roland also moved our aging tractor out of the top paddock and put it in the yard and covered it, to protect it from the worst of the weather. His final entry in the diary during his Christmas cover, on the 26th December reads as follows:-

'This has been an eye opening experience and Alison and I have really enjoyed working here. All the animals are in really good condition, so well done everyone.'

He re-iterated his earlier instructions that 'Time is to be spent on the horses, as they are almost feral. Not enough human contact. The time that was spent on filling hay nets and putting them up on shelters should now be spent working on the horses.'

We girls were very pleased at the changes Roland had made. He had approached the work in a completely different way and questioned the way we did things, which was good. We had done things the same way for ages and hadn't thought how we might make life easier for ourselves.

However, my worries were soon to come flooding back, as another blow was on the horizon. Early in 2018, Kelly suddenly announced she felt she could no longer continue to work at the sanctuary and left us. Martin also left. We were down to three. Micala, me and Angie.

Over the years, it has been tough to get used to new people, rely on them, get fond of them, then they leave. I am loathe to speak too soon and tempt fate, as I have seen so many people coming and going, but I think and hope, Micala will be a 'keeper'.

She was immediately made manager and quickly introduced some changes at the sanctuary. One of the first things she did was to buy new food supplements and she made changes to the feeding regime. Those who she feels need it have 'balancer' and 'Biotin' added to their feeds, which are full of vitamins and very good for hoof growth. We also apply Hoof Moist to those who need it, as this also helps hoof growth.

We continue to use 'Devil's Relief' which has stopped Haidi's joints creaking and Fie seems to be enjoying the benefits of this as well. Devils Relief is a powerful combination of herbal tinctures, formulated together with Devils Claw, which helps ease stiffness. Older horses benefit from this because the action of this formulation can help stimulate the older horses' digestion. I wonder if this works on humans!

Micala has continued to work with our most difficult horses, as you would have read in previous chapters. She has broken in Rudolph and Snowflake and Vera is now 'tamed'. Vera is now seen by the farrier regularly and is very calm during the process, something I thought I would never see.

Micala has recently married her fiancé, Wez and he has taken over the DIY and maintenance work at the sanctuary. They have recently introduced chickens and four sheep to the sanctuary. In addition, Micala has also rescued a young pony from the drift sales. Maybelle has formed a very strong attachment to Snowflake and has come to trust us in the few weeks she has been with us. Micala also has plans for a small allotment and maybe a few donkeys there. She and Wez spend a lot of their own time up there, which is good company for the horses.

For my part, I really appreciate the excellent communications between Micala and I. Like no manager before her, we are in regular contact and she includes me in decisions about the horses and I normally go up there to help when the farrier and dentist are on site. Due to the regular handling of all of our horses that she also insists on, my confidence around them has improved massively.

Thanks to her, our horses really are Now in Safe Hands.

ACKNOWLEDGEMENTS AND THANKS.

Thanks firstly go to my long suffering partner Terrina. She has had to put up with my passion for the sanctuary and the horses there and the roller-coaster ride of the ranges of emotions I have been through over the eight years I have worked at the sanctuary. In addition to that, she has had to listen to me rambling on about this book for years. Then she had to read and edit several versions of it, as it grew from the first day I started writing it in 2015, to the final manuscript.

For also reading my scripts and making suggestions for much needed enhancements and improvements, thanks go to Angie Tourle, friend and volunteer at the Sanctuary and also my friend Paul Wilkie. His painfully honest comments guided me to add depth, character, humour and warmth, which he felt were lacking in the early manuscripts.

The majority of the information on the horses has been provided by Roland and Alison, owners of the Devon sanctuary. So, many thanks go to them for putting together the information I asked for over the years and enduring my constant nagging, when I thought they were not providing the information I needed quickly enough. I once accused Roland of hiding behind his sofa when I rang him, pretending to be out, so another member of his family would have to take my call.

My other source of information came from the sanctuary diaries I could find, which were kept over the years. So I also want to thank the staff and volunteers for their comprehensive entries: Sian, Leanne, Micala, Kelly, Lara and Julie.

Finally, I thought I would never, ever get this published, so loads of thanks to Derek Hall, a graphic designer who formatted the manuscript and gave me a lot of advice and guidance during the process. Thanks also to David Parsons at Imprint Digital Publishers for his help and support. I would recommend that anyone who wants to self-publish should contact these people first.